INSTITUTIONAL EFFECTIVENESS AND OUTCOMES ASSESSMENT IMPLEMENTATION ON CAMPUS:
A Practitioner's Handbook

INSTITUTIONAL EFFECTIVENESS AND OUTCOMES ASSESSMENT IMPLEMENTATION ON CAMPUS:
A Practitioner's Handbook

by **James O. Nichols**
*Director, University Planning and
Institutional Research,
The University of Mississippi*

Resource Sections by

Gale Bridger, *Louisiana State University, Shreveport*
Marsha Krotseng, *University of Mississippi*
Linda Pratt, *North Carolina Central University*
Donald Reichard, *University of North Carolina at Greensboro*
Brenda Rogers, *North Carolina State University*
Bobby Sharp, *Appalachian State University*
Michael Yost, *Trinity University*

**Agathon Press
New York**

Library of Congress Cataloging-in-Publication Data

Nichols, James O. (James Oliver), 1941–
  Institutional effectiveness and outcomes
assessment implementation on campus.

  Includes bibliographies and index.
  1. Universities and colleges—United States
—Evaluation.   2. Universities and colleges
—United States—Accreditation.   I. Title.
LB2331.63.N53   1989   378.73   88-7626
ISBN 0-87586-089-3

Printed in U.S.A.

Contents

Preface and Acknowledgments

The emergence of assessment of student outcomes and institutional effectiveness as a significant trend in higher education during the last several years is evidenced in a number of ways, including the interest of the federal government, the activities of regional and professional accrediting associations, and the concerns expressed by governors and state legislatures. But because this is a relatively new trend, institutions that for one reason or another have decided to implement a program of institutional effectiveness or outcomes assessment are faced with the question, "How do we go about implementing these relatively theoretical concepts?"

The search for an implementation model is complicated by several factors. Institutions with national reputations in student outcomes or institutional effectiveness are often described as (a) unique, (b) being led by a Chief Executive Officer with a particularly keen interest in the subject, or (c) financially benefiting from implementation through their state funding formula and therefore able to invest heavily in the implementation process itself. Because these institutions are unique, their models of implementation seem irreplicable, which leaves more traditional two- and four-year institutions "reinventing the wheel" of outcomes assessment or institutional effectiveness implementation.

The search for an implementation model or plan is further complicated by the difficulty of adapting another institution's plan to the campus environment and the position of a number of accrediting associations. Institutional effectiveness or outcomes assessment, more than many other processes in higher education, must be tuned to each particular campus environment. Trying to "plug in" procedures used at another institution can be dangerous.

Regional and professional accrediting associations, under the guidance of the Council on Postsecondary Accreditation, have been among the leaders in the spread of outcomes assessment or institutional effectiveness implementation. However, these accrediting bodies, while willing to set institutional criteria for implementation results, have been in most cases understandably reluctant to specify *how* these mandates are to be met for fear of being accused of being "prescriptive" regarding internal institutional operations.

It became apparent in the summer of 1987 that (a) the national movement toward institutional effectiveness was continuing to gain momentum, (b) there were a number of institutions that were beginning implementation, and (c) the absence of a generalized model or plan for implementation was causing wasteful and potentially hazardous duplication of effort in designing implementation processes on many different campuses. At that time, the undersigned primary author and a number of colleagues who had (a) led successful outcomes assessment implementation on their own campuses, (b) played major roles in the authorship of accrediting association documents concerning outcomes assessment or institutional effectiveness, (c) pilot-tested accreditation association requirements concerning the subject, (d) served on accreditation teams with individual responsibility for outcomes assessment, (e) consulted widely in the field, or (f) were then actively involved in implementation activities, decided to pool their knowledge and experience in an effort to propose a general model or plan for implementation of institutional effectiveness and outcomes assessment.

It was determined that the implementation plan or model to be suggested should:

- Outline a general sequence of events leading toward genuine and comprehensive campus implementation of institutional effectiveness or outcomes assessment.
- Be adaptable to virtually every type of institutional circumstance.
- Require as small an amount of additional funding as possible by the institution.
- Be supported by detailed reviews of practice or literature in the field at the critical points of implementation.

The pages that follow were designed to meet these criteria. *The Practitioner's Handbook* is divided into three basic sections. Chapters I and II explain the *Handbook's* use and offer an overview of the institutional effectiveness or outcomes assessment implementation plan.

Chapters III through VII deal with the specific sequence of events or activities suggested during the course of four years in working toward comprehensive institutional implementation. These chapters are supported by six Resource Sections covering in greater depth more specific technical aspects of implementation. Finally, the third section of the *Handbook* offers examples at the institutional and departmental levels of institutional effectiveness implementation at a fictitious institution, "Our University." Overall, the *Handbook* is intended to provide the practical guidance needed for implementation as well as specific examples of that implementation.

It is important to understand that no work in this field will remain definitive in nature over a number of years. The field is growing rapidly, and with each passing year the experience base of institutions that have successfully implemented outcomes assessment or institutional effectiveness operations increases at a faster rate. In addition, the instrumentation (tests, surveys, etc.) available to support that implementation has been advanced substantially even during the course of the preparation of this document. Hence, the usefulness of this edition of the *Practitioner's Handbook* will be greatest for those institutions currently attempting implementation of outcomes or institutional effectiveness assessment. It is anticipated that in several years a subsequent edition of the *Practitioner's Handbook* will update both the proposed sequence of events and the more technical information supporting that implementation.

Acknowledgments

The Resource Section authors whose biographical sketches follow were asked to submit their material on an accelerated schedule, and each did so in a highly professional manner. I am indebted to them collectively and individually for the quality and promptness of their submissions as well as for their suggestions guiding the general development of the *Practitioner's Handbook:*

Gale W. Bridger is Associate Professor of Education and Associate Vice Chancellor for Academic Affairs at Louisiana State University (LSUS) in Shreveport. She serves as chief planning and evaluation officer for the university and coordinates the institutional research function. In 1981–82, Dr. Bridger was instrumental in establishing LSUS as a pilot institution for the Criteria (while still in draft stage) of the Southern Association's College Commission. Her institution has adopted a performance plan that includes multiple effectiveness meax   Preface and Acknowledgments

sures, all coordinated through her office. She is the immediate Past President of the Louisiana Association for Institutional Research and has served on several SACS visiting committees with primary responsibility for Criterion III: Institutional Effectiveness. She earned her doctorate in secondary education at The University of Mississippi in May 1974.

Marsha V. Krotseng is Institutional Research Associate and Assistant Professor of Higher Education at the University of Mississippi, where she is currently developing a "family" of student and alumni attitudinal surveys. Active in both the Association for Institutional Research and the Southern Association for Institutional Research, Dr. Krotseng has written a number of papers and served as a consultant on institutional effectiveness. She received her doctoral degree in higher education from the College of William and Mary in 1987.

Linda K. Pratt holds a Ph.D. in psychology from Texas Christian University. As the Associate Vice-Chancellor for Academic Affairs for Research, Evaluation and Planning at North Carolina Central University in Durham, N.C., she coordinates and monitors the planning system and oversees institutional research and academic evaluation activities. Previously she served at the National Laboratory for Higher Education where she wrote more than a dozen technical reports. Former President of the Southern Association for Institutional Research, she has also been active in the Association for Institutional Research, serving on the Professional Development Committee and the Nominating Committee and chairing the Workshop Committee. As a professor of psychology, she teaches and advises graduate students.

Donald J. Reichard has been Director of the Office of Institutional Research at the University of North Carolina at Greensboro since 1974. From 1970 to 1974, he was a Research Associate with the Southern Regional Education Board. His Ph.D. in higher education is from Michigan State University. In 1986–87, he served as President of The Association for Institutional Research. The title of his Presidential General Session Address at the 1987 AIR Forum in Kansas City (with Theodore J. Marchese) was "Assessment, Accreditation, and Institutional Effectiveness: Implications for Our Profession."

Brenda Hyde Rogers earned a Ph.D. in psychology from North Carolina State University where she holds an adjunct appointment and teaches tests and measurement. She served as Assistant Director of Institutional Research at North Carolina State University from 1983 to 1987 and is currently the Associate Director of the Office of Research, Evaluation and Planning at North Carolina Central University in Durham, N.C. She directed one of the seven student outcomes projects sponsored by NCHEMS/Kellogg and has written numerous papers and reports on student performance and institutional effectiveness that have been presented at national, regional and state conferences.

Bobby H. Sharp is Director of Institutional Research at Appalachian State University in Boone, North Carolina, where he also holds an academic appointment in the Department of Leadership and Higher Education. He earned a Ph.D. in Consumer Economics from Virginia Tech and holds other graduate degrees from the University of Kentucky and Duke University. His prior institutional research positions have included Associate Director of University Planning and Institutional Research at the University of Mississippi and Director of Institutional Research at the Mississippi University for Women. His research interests include decision support systems and modeling.

Michael Yost, Jr., has been at Trinity University, San Antonio, Texas, since 1971, and is currently Assistant to the President, Director of Institutional Research, and a tenured professor. He received his doctorate from Nova University, where he majored in research design, methodology and applied statistics. He is experienced in the development, implementation and evaluation of educational and institutional programs, statistical analysis, and computer applications. In recent years, he has worked with both private and public institutions. In the last twelve years, he has published more than 100 articles dealing with methodological and statistical applications. He has also made numerous professional presentations in the United States and in Europe and is presently a consultant to several universities and corporations.

In addition to these Resource Section authors, there is another group of individuals without whose work this publication would have been impossible. These are the staff within the Office of University Planning and Institutional Research at the University of Mississippi. They include Ms. Evelyn Spillers, who spent countless hours assisting in preparation of the manuscript, as well as Ms. Katherine Adams and Ms. Virginia Odle, who were of invaluable assistance in editing the work. In addition, Dr. Marsha Krotseng, the author of one of the Resource Sections, played a major role in preparation of the overall publication as well as the subject index. Finally, if the following document is readable and free of grammatical, spelling, punctuation, and similar errors, a major reason will be the contribution of Dr. Sharon Sharp, who served as our copy editor for the document. Sharon's close scrutiny improved all our work markedly.

Institutional effectiveness and outcomes assessment implementation is as dynamic a field as there currently is in higher education. Suggested practices today, in the light of further experience and improved instrumentation, are being improved almost overnight. Nonetheless, this first edition of the *Practitioner's Handbook* represents the most current and up-to-date material and suggestions available to a number of us in the field. It is respectfully offered for your consideration and use.

October 1988
James O. Nichols
Oxford, Mississippi

Endorsement of this publication has neither been sought nor received from any professional or regional accrediting association.

JAMES O. NICHOLS has been Director of University Planning and Institutional Research and Adjunct Assistant Professor of Higher Education at the University of Mississippi since 1979. He has been active in the field of institutional research and planning at a series of progressively more comprehensive institutions since 1971 and during that time served in leadership capacities in state, regional, and national professional associations. He currently serves on the Executive Committee of the Association for Institutional Research as Treasurer.

During the past four years, he has played a substantive role in the publication of regional accrediting association guidance regarding outcomes assessment; been a member of accreditation teams with specific responsibility for assessment of institutional effectiveness; presented national, regional, and statelevel workshops on institutional effectiveness implementation; and served as a consultant to more than a dozen institutions regarding outcomes assessment and institutional effectiveness implementation.

He received his Ph.D. in higher education from the University of Toledo in 1971 and since that time has made numerous contributions to the literature of higher education and the program at various professional meetings. In addition to this field, his major professional interests relate to college and university fiscal planning.

CHAPTER ONE

Explaining the Handbook's Use in Institutional Effectiveness and Outcomes Assessment Implementation

What can be expected from this publication?

The purpose of this *Handbook* is to provide a "cookbook" for the individual or group of persons on a college or university campus who have been given responsibility by the institution's Chief Executive Officer (CEO) for implementation of institutional effectiveness or outcomes assessment activities. As any good cook will admit, there is more than one way to prepare a stew, and that adage also holds true regarding institutional effectiveness and outcomes assessment activities. Presented in this handbook is one recipe that the author and his associates recommend as a starting point for implementation (cooking) activities. Individual cooks (practitioners) on each campus will naturally want to season or adapt this recipe to the taste (environment) of their own clientele (campus). There is no implication that the methodology proposed is the only manner through which such activities should be implemented.

How does this *Handbook* relate to other recent publications in the field?

This document is different in a number of ways from others that are currently being published in the field. First, it focuses almost exclusively on the *how* of institutional effectiveness or outcomes assessment rather than the *why*. For a variety of reasons—ranging from the perceived intrinsic value of the assessment of student educational outcomes (as a means for refinement of the educational process) to the more pragmatic reality of external forces (accrediting agency, state governments, etc.) requiring such actions—institutions across the country have already answered the why question and are now trying to determine how best to conduct such assessment. If your institution has not answered the why question in a clearly affirmative manner (for one reason or another), close this publication and devote your time to an activity that promises to be more productive. Unless an institution is clearly committed to institutional effectiveness or outcomes assessment at the beginning of process implementation, much energy will be expended with little genuine hope for meaningful impact on actual campus operations.

Second, this document attempts to be decidedly more practical than theoretical in its approach to the subject. Even when describing *how*, professional educators frequently slip into the glories of the cognitive and affective domains and other educational jargon. This document will touch upon such concepts strictly in laypersons' terms and move quickly to the more pragmatic means through which these concepts may be implemented on each campus.

This is a *handbook* rather than a scholarly work. In the body of the text, only sufficient references to credit primary sources will be found. However, in the six resource sections amplifying the body of the text, sufficient references to provide additional guidance concerning the various subjects are provided. For those interested in pursuing the subject of institutional effectiveness and outcomes assessment past the level of this document into a more scholarly treatment, the publication *Assessment of Outcomes for Accreditation*, by John Folger and John Harris, is recommended as a further primary source.

The *Handbook* is directed at the level of the practitioner rather than the Chief Executive Officer. Although the support of the Chief Executive Officer is absolutely essential to successful implementation, that support should have been gained in answering, Why do this? Also, the content of this document will be more detailed than one can reasonably expect a CEO to take time to digest. Undoubtedly, the practitioner or group whom the Chief Executive Officer has appointed to implement such activities will want to brief the CEO or explain to him or her the general outline of the implementation plan developed; however, this explanation should remain quite general unless requested otherwise or necessary to insure the CEO's support.

The proposed activities described lead toward long-term implementation of institutional effectiveness and outcomes assessment activities and not to a "quick fix" to the subject. Properly implemented, institutional effectiveness will take between 3 and 4 years to become fully operational. Although clear progress in specific activities required for full implementation of institutional effectiveness can occur rather quickly, the urge to "do something quick and easy" within a few months to satisfy an external agency will (in all likelihood) produce "something" so obviously superficial that it undermines the institution's opportunity for genuine progress toward substantive implementation over the longer period.

Finally, this *Handbook* describes a set of procedures for implementing **institutional effectiveness**, a concept that includes the assessment of student outcomes. However, institutional effectiveness extends beyond that important activity by placing the assessment of student outcomes as the focal point of an institution's commitment toward accomplishment of its statement of purpose.

The "assessment" movement sweeping through much of higher education is often focused at the departmental level within the academic components of an institution. These departmental outcomes assessment activities often seek to determine what students are learning in an effort to improve instructional methods or curricula. On some campuses, the results of the assessment of student outcomes or learning are compared to a departmental or program statement of expected or intended educational (instructional) outcomes. Although such assessment activities are laudable in their own right, in many instances they lack institutional-level commitment, and their continuation over an extended period of time may be questionable.

Institutional effectiveness, as described in more detail later in this chapter, raises the unit of analysis to the institutional level and incorporates assessment activities throughout the institution's instructional, research, and public service functions as well as its administrative components. Extension of the unit of analysis to the institutional level is accomplished by linkage of departmental statements of intended educational (instructional), research, and service outcomes, as well as administrative objectives, with an expanded statement of institutional purpose or mission. Verification that the institution's statement of purpose is being accomplished can be ascertained only through assessment results, which indicate that departmental/program intended outcomes (educational, research, and service) or objectives (administrative) are being accomplished. In this process, all components of the institution have a direct or indirect role to play in supporting or furthering accomplishment of the statement of purpose.

In summary, this document can be described as

1. Focusing primarily on the *how* in assessment and assuming that the question *why* has been answered;
2. Emphasizing the practical implementation of institutional effectiveness activities;
3. Constituting an administrative handbook rather than a scholarly work;
4. Being intended for the practitioner-level user;
5. Describing a long-term program of genuine implementation, rather than a "quick fix";
6. Including student outcomes assessment within an overall program of institutional effectiveness.

National Development of the Assessment (Institutional Effectiveness) Movement

It is difficult (and probably not worthwhile, given the purpose of this publication) to pinpoint the beginning of the current movement within the higher education community toward an emphasis on assessment. Suffice it to say that countless reports from national committees and commissions in the early to mid-1980s began calling for a renaissance in American higher education which would emphasize development of "excellence" in the outcomes or results of the educational endeavor. However, as often happens, this positive force toward reinvigoration and redirection began to shift its emphasis toward less altruistic ends.

By November 1985, the Secretary of Education was telling the American public through a speech before the American Council on Education that "Colleges should state their goals, measure their success in meeting those goals, and make the results available to everyone." He also stated, "If institutions don't assess their own performance, others—either states or commercial outfits—will most likely do it."

Although the apparent relationship with the more positive calls for excellence in the higher education community was retained, the emphasis had shifted to a more negative insistence on "measuring" results and the educational consumers' "rights" to review the results of that assessment. This shift was accompanied by the explicit threat of external intervention in institutional affairs if institutions didn't mend their ways.

Adding their voice to the call for increased assessment activities in higher education was the National Governors' Association. In their report *Time for Results: The Governors' 1991 Report on Education*, the governors called for all colleges and universities to develop comprehensive programs to measure student learning.

This action of the governors is being echoed by legislators and state governing boards. A survey of state governing/coordinating boards conducted in 1987 found that "all but a few of the state boards indicated that they were playing important roles in assessment; two-thirds could point to explicit statewide assessment programs planned or already in place" (Boyer, 1987). Further, the survey revealed "a basic change in attitude about the role of state boards, one that would not have been found even a few years ago. Governors and legislators have placed the quality of undergraduate education and student learning squarely on the state agenda. The state boards aim to keep it there" (Boyer, 1987).

Finally, the federal government has acted further to foster the concept of assessment through a proposal to change the "Secretary's Procedures and Criteria for Recognition of Accrediting Agencies," published in the *Federal Register* on September 8, 1987. The following two excerpts summarize the essence of Secretary William Bennett's proposal (*Federal Register*, 1987):

Explanation of Changes from Existing Procedures and Rules

The following is an explanation of the changes that would be made in existing procedures and rules by the proposed regulations.

Assessment of Student Achievement

There recently has been much emphasis within the postsecondary educational community on the effective assessment of student achievement as the principal measure of educational quality. The Secretary is in full accord with this trend and wishes to encourage it. Therefore, these revised regulations, in §602.17 in Subpart B, would place greater emphasis upon the consistent assessment of documentable student achievements as a principal element in the accreditation process. This emphasis would follow from an original justification for accreditation as the guarantor of the validity and reliability of educational degrees and credentials, and is in line with what Congress intended when it provided that the Secretary's recognition would help to assure that accrediting agencies were reliable authorities as to the quality of education or training offered.

The Secretary expects that accrediting agencies will respond to this emphasis on institutional quality as measured by student achievement in a variety of appropriate ways. Among other things the Secretary expects accrediting agencies to maintain full and accurate records. The Secretary invites comment about whether the provisions of this NPRM best ensure that accreditation standards and decisions reflect demonstrable student achievement.

§602.17 Focus on assessment of student achievement.

The Secretary determines whether an accrediting agency, in making its decisions, places substantial emphasis on the assessment of student achievement by educational institutions or programs, by requiring that each institution or program—

(a) Clearly specifies educational objectives that are appropriate in light of the degrees or certificates it awards;

(b) Adopts and implements effective measures, such as testing, for the verifiable and consistent assessment and documentation of the extent to which students achieve the educational objectives described in paragraph (a) of this section;

(c) Confers degrees or certificates only on those students who have demonstrated educational achievement as assessed and documented through appropriate measures described in paragraph (b) of this section;

(d) Broadly and accurately publicizes, particularly in representations directed to prospective students, the objectives described in paragraph (a) of this section, the assessment measures described in paragraph (b) of this section, and the information obtained through those measures; and

(e) Systematically applies the information obtained through the measures described in paragraph (b) of this section toward steps to foster enhanced student achievement with respect to the degrees or certificates offered by the institution or program. (Authority: 20 U.S.C. 1058 et al.)

This proposal generated a considerable amount of discussion among the various regional and professional accrediting associations and opened a candid dialogue concerning the proposal between the Council on Postsecondary Education (COPA) and the Department of Education. As of spring 1988, a revision in wording retaining the substance of the original proposal was being prepared in the Department of Education for release to Congress later in 1988. The importance of the proposed regulatory procedures is underscored by the realization that in order to receive most federal grants for student aid, research, and so forth, an institution must be fully accredited by an agency or accrediting body recognized by the Department of Education.

How has the higher education community responded to this pressure?

The primary response of the higher education community has been through that mechanism designed and established to perform the "quality assurance" role in higher education: regional and professional accrediting associations. In 1986 the Council on Postsecondary Accreditation, which coordinates the activities of virtually all accrediting agencies, issued a special report titled *Educational Quality and Accreditation*. This report recommends that educational institutions and programs "sharpen statements of mission and objectives to identify intended educational outcomes" and "develop additional effective means of assessing learning outcomes and results."

Even before this guidance from COPA, many regional (institutional) and professional (programmatic) accrediting agencies included some form or requirement for assessment activities as described in *Educational Quality and Accreditation*. However, renewed emphasis on outcomes assessment and substantive changes in accreditation processes among regional and professional accrediting associations have sprung from COPA's guidance, as well as from public pressure as voiced by federal and state officials.

Among the earliest national leaders responding to the call for increased assessment activities was the Commission on Colleges of the Southern Association of Colleges and Schools (SACS), which in 1985 passed a major change in its accrediting procedures in which outcomes assessment (or in SACS's terms, "institutional effectiveness") was identified on an equal basis with institutional processes in their *Criteria for Accreditation*. SACS consciously chose the term *institutional effectiveness* both to avoid the term *outcomes*, which many member institutions felt had become jargon-laden and had acquired undesirable connotations of "measuring everything that moves," and to indicate that the concept described was broader than assessment activities solely within an institution's academic departments.

The author and his associates have also chosen to utilize the term *institutional effectiveness* for the *Handbook*. This choice has been based upon the belief that while student outcomes assessment should be the central and most visible focus of the assessment movement, the longer-term success of that movement is contingent upon its integration and support at the institutional level on each campus. In addition, the term *institutional effectiveness* is more descriptive and inclusive of the identification of institutional and departmental programmatic intentions (as required by COPA) than is the term *outcomes assessment*.

What then are the common components of institutional effectiveness or outcomes assessment?

Although regional and professional accreditation requirements differ in terms of semantics, most call for those components identified by COPA: (a) a sharpened statement of mission and objectives, (b) identification of intended departmental/programmatic outcomes or results, and (c) establishment of effective means of assessing the accomplishment outcomes and results.

Added to this, implicitly, is the use of the assessment results obtained to improve the function of the institution or program (see Figure 1).

Figure I

Common Components Regarding Institutional
Effectiveness (Including Outcomes Assessment)
Found Among Accrediting Association Requirements

• A clear statement of institutional purpose, mission, goals, or objectives

• Identification of intended departmental/programmatic outcomes or objectives supporting accomplishment of the institutional statement of purpose

• Establishment of effective means for assessment of the extent to which departmental/programmatic outcomes or objectives have been accomplished

• Utilization of assessment results to improve or change institutional, programmatic, or departmental intentions or operations

The Institutional Effectiveness Paradigm

How then should an institution go about integrating these four institutional effectiveness components into its ongoing academic and administrative operations so that they become a part of its fabric? What assistance does the literature and practice in the field of higher education administration offer? What current practices can be adapted to incorporate these components? One answer to these questions is graphically portrayed in Figure 2, the **Institutional Effectiveness Paradigm**, and is described in the following explanation.

This paradigm depicts activities that have been proposed, fostered, and occasionally practiced by many authors and institutions for a number of years. It is an important adaptation of the rational planning model which has existed and been discussed in the literature during the past. Skeptics will quickly ask, Why this rational model when we know that campuses are essentially political entities and often act irrationally? The answer is that its elements precisely fit those components required by COPA and inherent in most accreditation processes. Others will then ask, How is *this* version of rational planning different from those that have been proposed and implemented, only to fail, before? The primary differences in implementation of this paradigm are its focus on assessment of results (as opposed to processes and resource requirements) and the fact that periodically representatives of our peers, and indirectly the public, are going to visit our campus to see if the components of institutional effectiveness are indeed being practiced as well as they are professed to be.

The critical elements of the Institutional Effectiveness Paradigm displayed in Figure 2, whose implementation is the subject of this *Handbook*, are as follows:

1. Establishment of an Expanded Statement of Institutional Purpose
2. Identification of Intended Educational (Instructional), Research, and Service Outcomes/Administrative Objectives
3. Assessment of the Extent to which the Intended Outcomes and Objectives Are Being Accomplished
4. Adjustment of the Institution's Purpose, Intended Outcomes/ Objectives, or Activities Based upon Assessment Findings

Almost from its inception, regional accreditation has focused upon accomplishment of the institution's "statement of purpose" or mission. Yet, today, the purpose or mission statements of most institu-

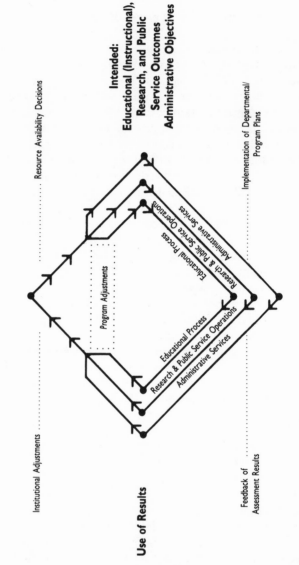

Figure 2
THE INSTITUTIONAL EFFECTIVENESS PARADIGM*

Expanded Statement of Purpose

Intended:
Educational (Instructional),
Research, and Public
Service Outcomes
Administrative Objectives

Resource Availability Decisions

Implementation of Departmental/
Program Plans

Institutional Adjustments

Program Adjustments

Educational Process
Research & Public Service Operations
Administrative Services

Educational Process
Research & Public Service Operations
Administrative Services

Assessment Activities

Use of Results

Feedback of
Assessment Results

*A related diagram was originated by the primary author and appeared in the Resource Manual on Institutional Effectiveness (1987).

tions are virtually interchangeable. Why is this the case? There are many reasons, but two are most apparent. First, accreditation procedures, up until this time, have been primarily episodic. Every 10 years, the institution's mission or statement of purpose has been studied by a faculty committee, reworded (usually retaining the same lack of substance), presented to the visiting committee, and afterward promptly filed and forgotten for another 10 years. Second, such disregard for the influence of the statement of purpose was possible because of the assumption (some would call it a "leap of faith") that if the institution could demonstrate adequate educational and administrative processes and financial resources, then surely it must be accomplishing its purpose. There are many other reasons, and the result has been the singular lack of meaning or importance to actual institutional functioning that characterizes most current statements of institutional purpose.

Institutional effectiveness (and outcomes assessment) is changing the role of the statement of purpose. Instead of "assuming" their accomplishments, institutions are being challenged to demonstrate their overall effectiveness through assessment of departmental/ program outcomes and objectives linked closely to the institution's statement of purpose. This requirement changes the mission or statement of purpose from a shelf-document with little practical use to the basis for institutional action that it was intended to be. In order to provide a useful basis for institutional effectiveness assessment, most existing statements of purpose must be substantially expanded and maintained to reflect institutional intentions. Further, a working relationship between the revised statement of purpose and the intended outcomes and objectives at departmental and program levels must be established.

Expansion and refinement of the institutional statement of purpose are described in more detail in Chapter 3 as an essential early element of implementing institutional effectiveness. A separate resource section within that chapter offers further guidance concerning means for establishment of such an "Expanded Statement of Institutional Purpose," and Appendix A contains an example of a statement.

Many aspects of an institution's expanded statement of purpose will require no additional funding, only adjustment of institutional policies. In the case of those components of the expanded statement of purpose that do require increased funding, the institution will be required to set its priorities among what will assuredly be more components and proposals than funds to support.

Actual implementation of the institution's expanded statement of purpose will, in most instances, take place at the departmental and program levels through the identification of intended outcomes and objectives linked closely to the expanded statement of purpose and focusing upon the institution's intended impact on its constituents or external environment. This intent will primarily consist of institutional assertions concerning its role regarding instruction, research, and public service. These institutional statements of intentions will primarily be implemented by the institution's academic units through identification of their own intended educational (instructional), research, and public service outcomes.

The institution's administrative departments also have a vital, if less direct or obvious, role to play in institutional effectiveness. Some expanded institutional statements of purpose will undoubtedly contain specific references to necessary support services (computer, library, counseling, etc.) as being essential to support of the institution's educational, research, and public service outcomes. In such cases, the institution's administrative departments will play a direct role and set objectives clearly related to the expanded statement of purpose. At other institutions, administrative units will not be as directly linked to the expanded statement of purpose but should establish objectives that they believe provide an administrative or physical environment conducive to accomplishment of the institution's expanded statement of purpose.

The formulation of statements of intended outcomes and objectives is described in Chapter 4 and its major resource section entitled "Setting Intended Educational (Instructional), Research, and Service Outcomes and Administrative Objectives." Appendix B contains examples of a number of such statements of intended outcomes or objectives linked with the example expanded statement of purpose contained in Appendix A.

Once the expanded institutional statement of purpose and departmental statements of intended outcomes and administrative objectives are in place, the institution (primarily through its departments) will implement activities to accomplish these ends (see Figure 2). Without much question, the single aspect of institutional effectiveness that has gained the highest level of public visibility, is *assessment*. Note that assessment, within the paradigm described, (a) occurs after establishment of the expanded statement of purpose and its supporting departmental or program statements of intended outcomes or administrative objectives, (b) is focused on ascertaining the extent of accomplishment of those outcomes and objectives identified, and (c) does attempt to assess every aspect of an institution's operations.

This controversial subject, assessment, is introduced in Chapter 4 and discussed in some detail in its accompanying major resource section entitled "Designing the Assessment Process."

Probably the most unnoticed—yet in the opinion of some, most important—elements of institutional effectiveness operations are the feedback or reporting of assessment findings and the use of such findings in adjusting institutional and departmental actions. This use will include potential adjustment of the expanded institutional statement of purpose, modification to departmental/program statements of intended outcomes and administrative objectives, and changes in departmental operations designed to accomplish the purposes intended.

The paradigm described and illustrated in Figure 2 is neither complex nor unfamiliar. The primary difference from earlier such paradigms lies in its focus upon results rather than processes or resources. Thus, implementation of this paradigm is of necessity ends, rather than means, oriented.

Implementation of the Institutional Effectiveness Paradigm

Although the Institutional Effectiveness Paradigm shown in Figure 2 relates the common requirements contained in most accreditation criteria (see Figure 1) to the literature and practice in higher education, it is apparent that implementation of the entire paradigm in a short period of time is not feasible on most campuses. This is true for the following reasons:

1. There is a clear sequential relationship between a number of the components (first purpose, then intended results, etc.).
2. Implementation in a short period (if possible) would leave little time for the institution's ongoing educational, research, and public service functions.
3. The nature of college and university governance requires participation and input by various constituents whose actions are relatively resistant to hasty action.
4. The fiscal implications of implementation of the paradigm in a short period could well be prohibitive.

How then does one go about implementing the Institutional Effectiveness Paradigm? The answer lies with the considerable thought, organization, and participation outlined in the next chapter and explained in the balance of this *Handbook*.

Scores of practitioners in various fields have observed as they have attempted to translate theory into practice, Nobody ever said this was going to be either easy or quick. Implementation of institutional effectiveness is no exception. Unlike Shakespeare's Macbeth, who approached his mission by musing, "If it were done when 'tis done, then 'twere well / It were done quickly," those who implement institutional effectiveness should do so carefully and thoroughly—or someone's corpse (career-wise) could be the result. The following suggested 4-year sequence of events is designed to accomplish substantive implementation of institutional effectiveness while offering a good chance for the survival of that individual or group therewith charged.

References: Cited and Recommended

Banta, T. (Ed.) (1988). *Implementing outcomes assessment*. New Directions for Institutional Research, No. 59. San Francisco: Jossey-Bass.

Bennett calls on colleges to assess their own performance, publish results. (1985, November 6) *Chronicle of Higher Education*, p. 25.

Boyer, C., Ewell, P., Finney, J. E., & Mingle, J. R. (1987). Assessment and outcomes measurement: A view from the states. *AAHE Bulletin, 39*(7), 8–12.

Council on Postsecondary Accreditation. (1986). *Educational quality and accreditation: A call for diversity, continuity, and innovation*. Washington, DC: Author.

Criteria for accreditation: Commission on Colleges. (1984). Atlanta, GA: Southern Association of Colleges and Schools.

Federal Register, Department of Education. (1987, September 8). *34CFR Parts 602 and 603, Secretary's procedures and criteria for recognition of accrediting agencies; Notice of proposed rulemaking*. Washington, DC: Government Printing Office.

Folger, J., & Harris, J. (1988). *Assessment of outcomes for accreditation*. Atlanta, GA: Southern Association of Colleges and Schools.

Jacob, M., Astin, A., & Avala, F. (1988). *College student outcomes assessment: a talent development perspective*. ASHE-ERIC (Higher Education Reports 1987, No. 7). Washington, D.C.: Association for the Study of Higher Education, 1987.

Kells, H. (1988) *Self-study process: a guide for postsecondary and similar service-oriented institutions and programs* (3rd ed.). New York: Macmillan.

Report of the Task Force on College Quality. (1986). *Time for results: The governors' 1991 report on education*. Washington, DC: National Governors' Association.

Resource manual on institutional effectiveness (1987). Atlanta: Commission on Colleges of the Southern Association of Colleges and Schools.

CHAPTER TWO

Overview of the Institutional Effectiveness Implementation Plan: Its Assumptions, Basis, and Execution

Assumptions and Management Decisions Supporting Plan Implementation

The *how* of institutional effectiveness and outcomes assessment is clearly the heart of this *Handbook*. However, it is important to understand the assumptions and basic plan management decisions that undergird the conduct of the implementation plan described later in this chapter. The implementation plan presented assumes the following:

1. *Institutional support for genuine implementation*—Nothing in this document provides a means through which to emphasize form rather than substance in institutional effectiveness implementation.
2. *Sensitivity of subject*—The most "sacred" activity in higher education is that which takes place behind the classroom door, and no effort should be made by the administration to dictate the instructional process.
3. *Limited additional funding for institutional effectiveness implementation*—Implementation will cost time and money; however, the expenditure of both should be limited as much as possible.

Probably the most important initial plan management decision or realization in implementation of institutional effectiveness is the need to appoint a single individual to coordinate the process. Why is this the case? First, implementation of institutional effectiveness will be a considerable effort ultimately impacting most aspects of the institution, and the nature of the work required will call for coordination and logistical support across departments and management levels. Second, implementation of institutional effectiveness is one project that, unlike class scheduling, registration of students, and the payroll, can be postponed unless there is an individual designated to continue moving (pushing) implementation toward culmination.

Who should be appointed to coordinate institutional effectiveness implementation? There is no best answer to this question that applies to all institutions. Three general sources for such leadership appear to be emerging on campuses:

1. Academician—Some institutions find that the credibility gained by appointment of an "interested" member of the faculty to head implementation is worthwhile, given the sensitivity of the subject.
2. Institutional researcher—Given the primarily quantitative nature of the assessment activity and the existence of an office with such expertise, a number of institutions have chosen to designate their institutional research officer to coordinate the implementation effort.
3. Institutional planner—Clearly the heart of institutional effectiveness is its relationship to campus planning efforts, and a number of institutions are choosing to emphasize the connection between institutional effectiveness and planning through appointment of a planning officer to coordinate the implementation effort.

Any of the type individuals just described can be successful in the coordinator's role, as long as there is recognition that it is this individual's responsibility to see that implementation across the institution is being accomplished or that the institution's leadership knows where and why not.

Although the coordinator selected will have central responsibility for implementation, exercise of that role will necessarily be through a team appointed for that purpose, and actual implementation will be the responsibility of the individuals in the institution's administrative and academic departments. There appear to be three institutional effectiveness roles emerging as part of the implementation team: the institutional planner, departmental facilitator, and assessment support person.

The Institutional Effectiveness Paradigm begins and ends with planning and assessment of the success of its implementation. A key role emerging is that of coordinating and supporting the planning processes of an institution from the highest level through the academic and administrative departments on the campus. Most authorities in the field of college and university planning stress the importance of linking the ideas expressed in campus plans with the actions taken through fund allocation, and this link between planning and budgeting must be visibly maintained. However, on many campuses this linkage has grown to the point that planning has become little more than a useful form of budgeting. The planning required by institutional effectiveness, although related to budget planning as a means, is distinctly more ends oriented and calls for an additional outcomes or results focus to planning at many institutions.

Academic and administrative departments will undoubtedly require further explanation of the concept and assistance in implementation of institutional effectiveness. The role of departmental implementation facilitator requires an individual with patience, credibility, and knowledge of institutional effectiveness to work with individual departments. Although such an individual cannot be expected to direct implementation within each department, he or she should explain the concept personally to each department (as it relates to their function), suggest a general course of action that the individual department might take toward implementation, and outline assessment options that are open to the department and are centrally supported.

Although the establishment of intended outcomes and objectives and (to a lesser degree) the conduct of assessment to determine if the intended ends have been accomplished are departmental responsibilities, a clear need exists for a centralized assessment support entity. This functionary (on many campuses the Office of Institutional Research) can provide (a) the assessment expertise needed to assist departments, (b) the logistical means for most efficiently conducting standardized testing and distributing/processing attitudinal instruments, and (c) a centralized point or clearinghouse for assessment results.

Probably the second most-asked set of questions concerning institutional effectiveness (after how) relates to the cost and source of funding. Several basic points related to this subject need to be made:

1. There are clearly increased costs involved, both direct (out-of-pocket expenditures) and indirect (time).
2. The amount of additional direct cost incurred on each campus will be dependent upon the institution's current activities (its existing

level of expenditures for planning, institutional research, etc.), the nature of the assessment plan adopted, the size of the institution, and the extent to which the costs incurred are passed on to students through fees for testing. Hence, a cost estimate will be difficult until a number of policy issues are settled and an inventory of existing assessment assets is conducted.

3. Many current institutional examples of successful outcomes assessment operations are the result of external grants for this purpose or state funding mechanisms (formulas) that have been altered to encourage and reward such activity. Regretably, these sources will not be available to most institutions as they go about institutional effectiveness implementation.

4. Initial funding for implementation should be relatively open-ended, although justified and carefully monitored.

Given the preceding comments, institutions are best advised first to acknowledge that implementation of institutional effectiveness will require additional expenditures for which they probably will not receive increased funding, and then to begin implementation activities by funding such implementation from contingency or discretionary funds available at the highest levels of the institution until a number of policy-level decisions are made and historical cost data are available at the institution.

Overcoming campus inertia and encouraging institutional effectiveness implementation will take decisive action on the part of the institution's CEO and the establishment of incentives for departmental cooperation. The CEO must not only support implementation but also openly evidence that support. Most CEOs will make the expected verbal endorsement of institutional effectiveness implementation; however, it is their actions that will (or will not) convince those on the campus of their sincerity. Among the actions that a CEO may take to demonstrate visibly his or her support for implementation are

1. Taking an active (though not dominant) role in preparation of the Expanded Statement of Institutional Purpose;
2. Establishing his or her office's administrative objectives supporting the expanded statement of purpose;
3. Contributing to the formulation of his or her discipline's statements of intended educational, research, or public service outcomes;
4. Referencing assessment results in public statements.

At the departmental level there also must be incentives toward implementation. Probably the best incentive is the intrinsic value inherent in the concept of institutional effectiveness and the improvement of student learning. However, other more extrinsic (and some would say material) means such as the following may be necessary:

1. Incorporation of institutional effectiveness implementation into the reward system (rank, tenure, etc.) for faculty
2. Provision of funding preferences within the institution to departments implementing institutional effectiveness
3. Increase of institutional visibility for those departments actively and effectively pursuing implementation

The Plan for Implementation of Institutional Effectiveness and Assessment Activities

Figure 3 contains a plan or sequence of activities for implementation of institutional effectiveness over a 4-year period based upon the assumptions and plan management decisions reviewed earlier in this chapter. Following the "Decision to Implement Institutional Effectiveness and Assessment Activities," events in the plan are portrayed as developing simultaneously down separate, but closely related, planning/operational and assessment/evaluation activities tracks.

Building the Necessary Institutional Foundation

During the first year of implementation, most activity of a planning/operational nature will be focused on "Establishment of an Expanded Institutional Statement of Purpose" as a foundation for further activities. The "Implementation of Attitudinal Surveys" and the "Conduct of an Inventory of Assessment Procedures" (as currently being employed at the institution or available to the institution) highlight the assessment/evaluation activities during the first year of implementation, which can be described as **Building the Necessary Institutional Foundation**. This first year of implementation activities is discussed in detail in Chapter 3, and four resource sections are provided to expand upon the most important concepts contained in that chapter.

Detailed Design at the Departmental Level

The second year of implementation is characterized as **Detailed Design at the Departmental Level**, during which time the work accomplished the previous year at the institutional level will be ex-

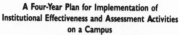

Figure 3

**A Four-Year Plan for Implementation of
Institutional Effectiveness and Assessment Activities
on a Campus**

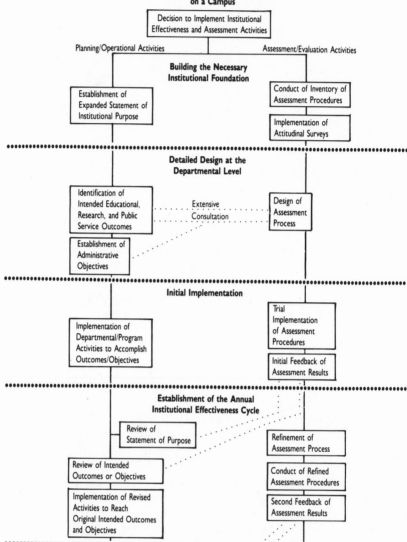

REPEAT FOURTH-YEAR ACTIVITIES—CONDUCT COMPREHENSIVE
INSTITUTIONAL AND PROCESS EVALUATION IN EIGHTH YEAR

● ● ● End of Implementation Year

tended to the departmental level. Planning/operational activities during the second year include the "Identification of Intended Educational, Research, and Public Services Outcomes" and the "Establishment of Administrative Objectives," both of which are closely linked with, and support accomplishment of, the expanded statement of purpose developed during the first year of implementation. These important statements of intended outcomes and objectives are closely coordinated with the "Design of the Assessment Process," through which accomplishment of these intentions will be evaluated. Second-year activities are described in Chapter 4, which includes two resource sections further explaining departmental outcomes/objectives and the design of an assessment process.

Initial Implementation

During the third year of implementation activities, the **Initial Implementation** of institutional effectiveness operations takes place. Based upon their work during the previous year, the institution's components will be involved in "Implementation of Departmental/ Program Activities to Accomplish Intended Outcomes/Objectives." The primary events during this third year will be the "Trial Implementation of Assessment Procedures," as designed during the previous year, and the "Initial Feedback of Assessment Results," as described in Chapter 5.

Establishment of the Annual Institutional Effectiveness Cycle

Establishment of the Annual Institutional Effectiveness Cycle is brought about in the fourth year of implementation activities and is described in Chapter 4. In that year, and each succeeding year, planning and operational activities will include "Review of the Statement of Purpose," "Revision of Intended Outcomes or Objectives," and/or "Implementation of Revised Activities to Reach Original Intended Outcomes and Objectives." Likewise, during each year in the annual cycle, "Refinement of the Assessment Process," "Conduct of Refined Assessment Procedures," and "Feedback of Assessment Results" will take place.

Why can't institutional effectiveness be implemented faster?

Some institutions, based upon their existing planning and institutional research activities, may be able to shorten the institutional effectiveness implementation plan by 6 months to a year. However, because most existing planning and institutional research functions are designed to support process-type decisions (budgeting, class scheduling, etc.), rather than assessment, the majority of institutions will require the full amount of time to complete implementation. The primary reasons for the lengthy period of time required for implementation are related to the assumptions regarding implementation enumerated earlier in this chapter.

Genuine implementation of institutional effectiveness will change the manner in which many institutions operate. A change of this magnitude cannot be brought about in a short period without creating massive resistance to not only the substance of the change but also the rapidity of the process of change.

In the academic area, institutional effectiveness deals with the most sensitive prerogatives of the faculty, those related to control of the curriculum and the classroom. Although there is absolutely no intention for institutional effectiveness to infringe upon these prerogatives, an attempt to rush or force implementation may very well be viewed as such by many faculty. Faculty participation in curriculum design and assessment of the accomplishment of intended outcomes is essential to successful genuine implementation of institutional effectiveness.

Acceleration of the process of implementing institutional effectiveness would require more personnel commitment (although over a shorter period) and higher out-of-pocket costs than most institutions can tolerate over a short period. Most institutions of higher learning do not have extra personnel who can readily be diverted to developmental tasks such as implementation of institutional effectiveness. Implementation will require a considerable amount of time on the part of various committees and most certainly within the academic and administrative departments as they identify intended outcomes and objectives as well as the means for their assessment. Frankly, there is a limited amount of "extra" service that faculty can be asked to assume over a short period, in addition to teaching, research, and service. However, extended over the longer period of the proposed plan, this level of involvement is distinctly feasible.

Likewise, rapid escalation of direct out-of-pocket expenditures to support institutional effectiveness will not be feasible at most institutions. Rather, gradual escalation of funding to meet documented needs for activities will be found both more feasible and more acceptable to others on the campus over the longer period of time suggested.

If genuine institutional effectiveness implementation were either easy or quick, more successful examples would be available. On the other hand, careful, well-planned implementation stands a far greater chance for substantive success and continuation over a period of years.

What will be the greatest problems encountered in executing the proposed institutional effectiveness implementation plan?

The problems will, of course, vary from campus to campus, but three of the most likely are (a) gaining the genuine commitment of the institution's administrators,(b) dealing with faculty resistance, and (c) maintaining momentum during the period of implementation.

Although verbal commitment (i.e., lip service) to institutional effectiveness implementation will come relatively easily from most administrators, follow-through into sustained support demonstrated by their actions may be another matter. For those not truly committed to the intrinsic value of institutional effectiveness, the key to their sustained support may lie in the extent to which they each become personally identified with the implementation effort and cannot afford to have it fail without reflection upon themselves.

Faculty resistance will arise during the implementation process. Such resistance will take forms varying from open resistance from faculty stating that nothing they intend to accomplish is subject to "measurement," to more serious passive resistance which may be found in departments that refuse to implement. In both cases, patience is the key to successful implementation. When gently pressed, even the most vocal faculty member must admit that *some* of the things his or her discipline intends to accomplish are ascertainable or observable over time. From that admission, the reluctant faculty member will often gradually accept institutional effectiveness implementation rather than risk a loss of credibility with his or her colleagues as a reasonable member of the community of scholars.

The department that passively resists implementation is a more serious problem, yet one that also is subject to being overcome with patience. Short of a change in leadership, which ultimately may be necessary, probably the best course of action is the structuring of the individual and departmental reward systems to make it abundantly clear that cooperation in implementation is in the best interest of those involved.

Probably the single greatest problem likely to be experienced with the implementation plan proposed is the maintenance of campus commitment and momentum over the 4-year period. On those campuses motivated toward implementation of institutional effectiveness to satisfy accreditation requirements, the leverage provided by this activity will help to sustain momentum. On other campuses it will be necessary to arrange events, activities, announcements, and so forth that emphasize the continuing importance of institutional effectiveness implementation, what has been accomplished to date, and the current activities and where they support final implementation.

Summary

In this chapter the essential components of and sequence of events for the proposed plan for implementation of institutional effectiveness have been very briefly outlined, as well as the assumptions upon which that plan is based and the plan management decisions that will need to be made. Finally, problems that the practitioner is likely to encounter during implementation have been identified. In the next several chapters, more detailed explanations of activities proposed during each year of institutional effectiveness implementation are presented.

CHAPTER THREE

Building the Necessary Institutional-Level Foundation for Institutional Effectiveness: the First Year

Following the institution's initial "Decision to Implement Institutional Effectiveness and Assessment Activities," the first year of implementation activities will be focused upon accomplishing the necessary homework to support the balance of the effort during the following 3 years. The first year's work, as shown in Figure 4, is based upon the assumptions that

1. There has been a visible and genuine campus commitment to institutional effectiveness implementation;
2. Adequate, though not unlimited, resources have been made available to begin implementation;
3. An individual has been named to assume leadership for coordination of overall institutional effectiveness implementation;
4. Team members with responsibility for institutional planning, departmental activity facilitation, and assessment (data gathering) have also been identified, along with an appropriate advisory group composed of representatives of a cross section of campus constituencies (see Figure 5);
5. Basic institutional process-oriented data (enrollment, teaching loads, average salary, etc.) designed to support ongoing decision making at the institution are available.

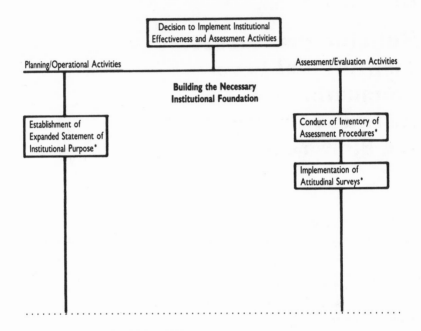

Figure 4

**The First Year of a Four-Year Plan for
Implementation of Institutional Effectiveness
and Assessment Activities on a Campus**

*Resource Section included in chapter to support

Within the first year, and in each of the succeeding years, implementation activities will be conducted along the separate, but related, planning/operational and assessment/evaluation activities tracks illustrated in Figure 4.

Planning/Operational Activities

Planning/operational activities undertaken during the first year of implementation include adaptation of the generic implementation plan provided to the specific institution and the formulation of an expanded institutional mission statement.

Figure 3, "A Four-Year Plan for Implementation of Institutional Effectiveness and Assessment Activities on Campus" (see p. 10)

Figure 5

The Institutional Effectiveness Implementation Team

Chief Executive Officer

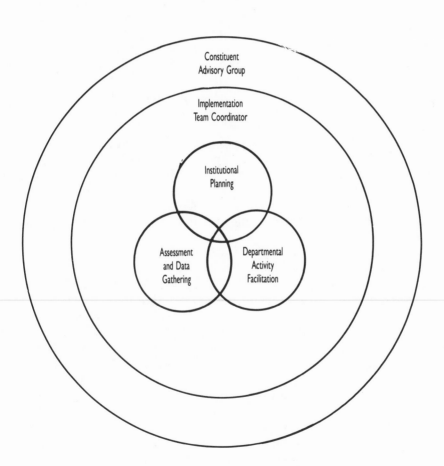

contains a depiction of the generalized or generic approach to implementation that forms the basis of this *Handbook*. However, it is important to realize that this approach will need to be adapted to specific institutional circumstances. Based upon the existing situation, some institutions may be able to compress somewhat the process of implementation because of the prior existence of certain components (e.g., an enhanced or expanded mission statement) on their campus. Other institutions will find it necessary to extend the process or commit additional resources to offset initial deficiencies (e.g., lack of basic process-oriented institutional data). The implementation plan depicted in Figure 3 should be modified to incorporate institution-specific terms, adjustments in estimated times, and specific dates by which activities should be completed on each campus. If implementation is in response to accreditation requirements, the institution will also want to ensure that the specific jargon (*outcomes, expected educational results*, etc.) utilized by the accrediting association is also included in the adaptation.

The primary task along the planning/operational activities track during the first year of implementation is "Establishment of an Expanded Statement of Institutional Purpose." This is one of the single most important actions in implementation of institutional effectiveness operations. As stated in Chapter 1, the key difference between outcomes assessment for its own sake and institutional effectiveness is the purposeful manner in which assessment is focused upon intended departmental/program outcomes or objectives linked to the Expanded Statement of Institutional Purpose in institutional effectiveness. This linkage is illustrated in Figure 6, and an understanding of it is essential to the concept of institutional effectiveness.

The Expanded Statement of Institutional Purpose is, then, the beginning and the end of the Institutional Effectiveness Paradigm shown in Figure 2. It provides the sense of direction or institutional intention that is supported by the statements of "Intended Educational, Research, and Public Service Outcomes" and "Administrative Objectives" identified by the academic and administrative departments. Ultimately, it is the extent to which these departmental/ program outcomes or objectives have been reached that is reflective of accomplishment of the Expanded Statement of Institutional Purpose.

The term *Expanded Statement of Institutional Purpose* has been chosen for two reasons. First, implementation of institutional effectiveness and outcomes assessment operations greatly expands and enhances the role of the document(s) as a guide to institutional priorities and

Figure 6

Relationship and Key Linkages between Expanded Statement of
Institutional Purpose, Intended Outcomes or Objectives, and Evaluation
in Institutional Effectiveness

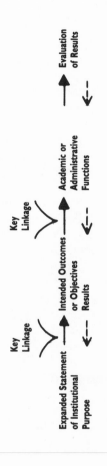

Expanded Statement
of Institutional
Purpose

Key
Linkage

Intended Outcomes
or Objectives
Results

Key
Linkage

Academic or
Administrative
Functions

Evaluation
of Results

Consistency in institutional direction or purpose
Evaluation of accomplishment of institutional purpose through departmental/program intended outcomes/objectives evaluation

operations. Second, the actual composition of the statement of purpose currently in existence at most institutions will need to be reviewed and substantially expanded. Many terms can be utilized to identify and structure such a statement (*mission, role and scope, purpose, goals, philosophy*, etc.), but the important concept to grasp is that the document(s) serving as the campus's Expanded Statement of Institutional Purpose should provide a clear and unequivocal statement of institutional-level intentions for the future so that departmental/ program statements of intentions may be directly linked to such institutional-level intentions.

Given the importance of the Expanded Statement of Institutional Purpose, how does an institution go about establishment or expansion of its statement of purpose? The answers are clearly as numerous as the institutions that must accomplish this delicate task. However, in the resource section entitled "Developing the Expanded Statement of Institutional Purpose," beginning on page 34, the author reviews the past and future roles of such statements, indicates desirable characteristics of such statements, discusses the possible role of strategic planning in this effort, and offers a potential action plan (subject to institutional adaptation) for accomplishing this task.

Finally, Appendix A contains an example of an Expanded Statement of Institutional Purpose which offers sufficient substance for use as a basis for institutional effectiveness operations on a campus.

Assessment/Evaluation Activities

Two major activities regarding assessment/evaluation (see Figure 4) should take place during the initial year of implementation: (a) conduct of an inventory of existing and available assessment procedures on the campus and (b) implementation of attitudinal surveys.

The "Conduct of an Inventory of Assessment Procedures" on the campus is clearly the place to begin along this track and will undoubtedly produce surprising results on most campuses. Among these surprising results will be the realization of how much assessment activity is already taking place in many of the institution's academic departments. Although the quality of the assessment-related activities found to be taking place will vary widely, there will probably be instances of truly excellent assessment activities already in place which can be utilized as examples to the rest of the institution's academic departments.

What are some of the types of assessment/evaluation activities that may already exist on your campus? You may find activities such as the following:

1. Entrance examinations—Although such examinations are not designed specifically to measure achievement at your institution, they are useful in establishing the level of academic competency of your entering students, from which your own accomplishments can be judged.

2. Standardized and locally prepared tests of graduating students— Although your institution may not require such testing of student knowledge (cognitive learning), some academic departments continue to administer or require such examinations. At least one national testing firm (Educational Testing Service) provides summary data regarding test scores to the institutions from which those students who took the examination reported receiving their degrees. In a separate resource section entitled "Cognitive Assessment Instruments: Availability and Utilization," beginning on page 65, the advantages, disadvantages, and costs of both locally designed and standardized cognitive examinations are reviewed.

3. Licensure examinations—Among the best end-of-program assessment procedures, already widely implemented in various disciplines, are licensure-type examinations such as those in accountancy, nursing, and law.

4. Departmental alumni follow-ups—Many departments attempt to stay in touch with their graduates and have received comments regarding their programs from that source.

5. Existing institutional data systems—Among the most frequently overlooked sources of assessment information is the institution's automated data system. Although most such data systems are likely to be designed for support of transactional (registration, fee payment, payroll, etc.) activities or, at best, process-type decision support (teaching loads, average salaries, space utilization, etc.), their potential for support of assessment is considerable. A resource section concerning this subject and entitled "Assessment-Related Information from Institutional Data Systems" is provided in this chapter and begins on page 81.

The process of conducting this initial inventory of existing and available assessment mechanisms should result in a comprehensive directory of existing assessment procedures and results. It should also result in a similar listing and analysis by discipline of those nationally available procedures (primarily standardized tests) that are not currently utilized on the campus.

The other major assessment/evaluation activity undertaken during the first year of implementation should be "Implementation of Attitudinal Surveys." The attitudes of an institution's constituents, including current and former students, employers, and the general public, are one important barometer of the extent to which an institution's purpose is being communicated and how accomplishment of that purpose is perceived. Some institutions and individual departments may already be utilizing separate survey instruments. However, it is unlikely that such instruments are focused upon soliciting responses directly related to the accomplishment of the Expanded Statement of Institutional Purpose or linked to departmental/program intended outcomes or objectives. This first year is an ideal time to initiate implementation of a family of attitudinal surveys to be focused specifically on these subjects.

A resource section entitled "Attitudinal Surveys in Institutional Effectiveness" is provided to further explore this subject as part of this section. It begins on page 48 and includes a discussion of (a) the types of attitudinal surveys, (b) various commercial instruments available for this purpose, (c) the local design or adaptation of attitudinal surveys, and (d) the benefits gained through centralization of processing such surveys while decentralizing the design process and emphasizing effective feedback of the results to the departmental/program level.

Complete implementation of attitudinal surveys will not be feasible until an Expanded Statement of Institutional Purpose and departmental/program statements of intended outcomes and objectives are finalized by the end of the first and second years of the implementation plan, respectively. However, most survey and feedback design work can be completed parallel to these actions. By the end of the first year, pilot testing of the instruments can be accomplished, and their phased implementation can be initiated.

Summary

By the close of the first year of implementation activities, the foundation should have been laid and the tools gathered for constructing institutional effectiveness operations on the campus. The document(s) serving as the Expanded Statement of Institutional Purpose should be in place to guide planning/operational activities throughout the next 3 years. The completed campus "Conduct of Inventory of Assessment Procedures" and initial "Implementation of Attitudinal

Surveys" serve to initiate identification and use of the means for assessment. Each of these actions at the institutional level supports a change in the focus of implementation activities to the department/ program level in the second year of implementation of institutional effectiveness on the campus.

Developing the
Expanded Statement of
Institutional Purpose

Michael Yost

In the preceding chapters the Expanded Statement of Institutional Purpose (ESIP) has been described as a key—if not the most important—part of assessing institutional effectiveness. This document or collection of documents is developed in much the same way that an architect develops the blueprint for a new building; and as the blueprint gives direction to those who construct the building, the ESIP gives direction to those who work at a college or university. In the pages that follow we describe the content of the ESIP, give examples of the content, describe how to construct the ESIP, and discuss the linkage between the content of the ESIP and the operation of the institution.

The ESIP should be thought of as being made up of two separate but related parts. The first of these parts is the statement of institutional mission, and the second is the statement of institutional goals. Collectively, these two documents give direction to the overall operation of the institution and clearly identify its intentions. The regional accrediting agencies in the United States require that all institutions have a mission statement which is valid and up-to-date. As a part of the process of developing an institutional effectiveness program for an institution, this document must be evaluated and updated.

The process of assessing institutional effectiveness is based upon perceived accomplishment of the institution's stated purpose as reflected in its ESIP. Because the institution is encouraged to formulate departmental/program statements of intentions consistent with the institution's purpose, great clarity and specificity in the statements of institutional intentions comprising the ESIP are needed. Although an institutional mission statement need not reach an operational level of detail, it should include sufficient substance to provide a clear framework for subsequent statements of institutional goals, thus providing a clear sense of direction for the institution's departmental statements. The ultimate determination of institutional effectiveness is in relation to the statement of purpose, and the demonstration of institutional effectiveness is through the accomplishment of institutional goals and departmental/programmatic results that are clearly linked to the institution's stated purpose.

Let us begin this process by examining the parts of an institutional mission statement. To assist in the writing of this *Handbook*, an example ESIP containing an institutional mission and goals statement has been developed for an institution referred to as "Our University." This document is located in Appendix A beginning on page 165, and portions are cited in the text of this resource section.

How long should an institutional mission statement be? As a part of the research in preparing to write this *Handbook*, statements of purpose or institutional intentions from many institutions were reviewed. The institutional mission statement is usually included as the first major topic in the catalog or bulletin of an institution. Typically, this document was found to be between one and three single-spaced, typed pages in length. The institutional mission statement usually begins with a statement such as the following:

> Our University is an independent, nonsectarian, coeducational institution, in the tradition of the liberal arts and sciences. Seeking to be faithful to ideals of its heritage, Our University is committed, in all of its policies and practices, to the unrestricted and rigorous pursuit of truth, to the certainty of values in human life, and to a respect for differing points of view.

This opening statement provides a brief history and philosophy of the institution, states whether it is privately or publicly supported, whether it is coeducational, and what the institution represents. This portion of the mission statement for Our University is somewhat shorter than it is for most institutions.

Another part of the institutional mission statement describes the type of student that the institution enrolls and the geographic area from which they come; for example:

> Our mission is to provide an outstanding education for a relatively small number of talented and highly motivated students from a diversity of geographic, ethnic, and socioeconomic backgrounds.

The first part of this statement describes the clientele (highly motivated, talented, with diverse ethnic and socioeconomic backgrounds), the size of the institution (relatively small), and the geographic area that the institution seeks to serve (diverse geographic backgrounds). This statement would have been written very differently if Our University were an institution supported by city, county, or state funds with defined geographic service boundaries.

The next section of the mission statement deals with the faculty.

> To achieve this end, we recruit and retain outstanding faculty members who are dedicated to the art of teaching and advising; to the search for and dissemination of truth through scholarship, research, and creative endeavor; and to service to the university and the larger community.

This statement describes all of the major activities engaged in by faculty members. These include teaching, advising, research (or creative activities), dissemination of information, and service. Many institutions place emphasis on one or more of these areas.

The academic environment is described in the next statement.

> We also seek to provide a supportive and challenging environment in which students can realize the full potential of their abilities and come to understand their responsibility of service in the human community.

This type of academic environment is good for an institution that emphasizes the liberal arts and sciences. However, if Our University were an engineering school or an occupationally oriented type of institution, this statement would have been written very differently.

Because the major business of institutions is to educate students, the description of the curriculum is one of the key elements of the institutional mission; for instance:

> The principal focus of Our University's curricular programs is undergraduate education in the liberal arts and sciences, combined with a number of preprofessional fields. Relations between the liberal arts and the preprofessional fields are carefully nurtured to provide mutually reinforcing intellectual experiences for students and faculty. Our University also offers master's and doctoral degree programs in selected professional areas that will prepare individuals for positions of leadership in their chosen careers.

For a relatively small institution that has a tightly focused curriculum, this statement can be very concise and relatively short. As the curriculum becomes more diverse, the amount of explanation required in the mission statement is greatly expanded. There are two points in the example that are noteworthy. First, the statement clearly defines the "principal focus" of the curriculum and, second, it states the relationship between the programs. These are both important ingredients of the institutional mission statement.

All public, and the majority of private, institutions have a sense of responsibility for providing some level of service to the community in which they are located. This service can take the form of faculty/staff participation in community events or nonuniversity events that take place on the university campus. In any event, if an institution does assume a public service role, it should be described in the institutional mission statement.

> In addition, recognizing its responsibility to the larger community, Our University provides a variety of carefully selected programs of continuing education and cultural enrichment.

Although some of the faculty at almost all institutions engage in research or other creative academic endeavors, not all institutions assume the responsibility of developing and maintaining a research program. Typically, relatively small institutions do not have research programs and large institutions do. Much of the decision as to whether or not to have such a program is a function of faculty, staff, equipment, space, and funding. In the event that an institution assumes a research function, it should appear as a part of the institutional mission statement.

> Finally, Our University recognizes its responsibility in maintaining a position of excellence and leadership in research.

It is difficult to believe that the administration and staff of an institution would exclude any individual enrollment or employment because of sex, race, religion, or national origin. Along with the moral issues associated with discrimination, there are many state and federal laws that forbid it. Because many individuals (students and employees) read the institutional mission statement, it is wise to include the institution's nondiscrimination statement in the mission statement.

In its recruitment and retention of members of the university community, Our University, consistent with its academic and institutional heritage, maintains an openness to all qualified persons.

The sample nondiscrimination statement is a shortened form of the legal version published by the federal government.

Because the institutional mission statement defines the most fundamental criteria for assessing institutional effectiveness, it serves several important functions. It (a) provides guidance for administrative decisions regarding the overall direction of the institution; (b) provides direction to each of the colleges, divisions, and departments of the institution, creating an umbrella under which those units may plan, operate, and evaluate their programs; and (c) establishes a general blueprint for the development of processes for assessing and improving institutional effectiveness. For these reasons, it is impossible to overstate the value and usefulness of statements of purpose which articulate the institution's commitment to important outcomes for students.

Developing the Institutional Mission Statement

Given the importance attached to the institutional mission statement, a significant task for each institution is to do the research needed to formulate that critical document. The potential approaches are, of course, as numerous as the institutions that must undertake the task. Assuming a broad perspective, much of the current literature in the field of higher education describes the general process of deriving the institutional mission statement as "strategic planning." Numerous writers (Cope, 1981; Keller, 1983; Shirley, 1982, 1983) have provided descriptions of the process, and although procedures suggested vary widely, these major authorities appear to agree on a number of important concepts. Strategic planning is an ends-oriented approach to planning which seeks to answer the questions What is the business of the institution? and How does the institution fit into an educational picture of the city, region, state, or country? It focuses on assessment of the institution's internal strengths and weaknesses and the institution's fit with or niche in the external educational environment. Although various techniques may be used, the result of this assessment is identification of environmental opportunities that are a good match for the strengths of the institution. An assessment of the institution's internal strengths and weaknesses is a major component of strategic planning. Whether this assessment is informal or formal, oral or written, focused more on strengths or more on weaknesses, the findings are critical in planning for the future.

The result of strategic planning is a clear sense of institutional direction resulting from conscious decisions about the role of the institution. The ongoing objective is the creation of a match among environmental opportunities, institutional values, and institutional strengths, coupled with resources available to support action in high-priority areas.

Now, let's consider an example of the application of strategic planning to Our University. Suppose that Our University had survived for nearly 100 years as a relatively small, private institution that had not undergone a great deal of change or reform. Suppose, further, that the institution was well endowed, and that it had a local and regional reputation of being a "good" institution, but one that didn't appear to have any outstanding academic programs. The physical plant was in good condition, the budget was balanced, and enrollment was stable and at an acceptable level. The members of the board of trustees, after hiring a new president, decided that the mission of the institution should be reviewed and, if necessary, changed.

At this point in time, the data required to support the evaluation of the existing mission (and possibly to support the development of a new mission) were gathered. Historic data indicated that the existing mission statement had not been evaluated since the last regional self-study, and that at that time there was only a cursory review of the mission. Also, since the last review of the mission statement, there had been several changes in the administrative structure of the institution, and several academic programs had been implemented that didn't appear to fit within the existing curriculum and mission. The new president suggested that a study be conducted to determine whether it would be feasible for the "principal focus of Our University's curricular programs to be undergraduate education in the liberal arts and sciences, combined with a number of preprofessional fields."

With this potential mission in mind, studies of internal strengths and weaknesses and external market constraints were undertaken. An examination of the external market constraints indicated that the nearest institution with this type of curricular offering was almost 500 miles away; high school students in the city and region were traveling outside of the region to attend schools with this type of curricular offering; on a national basis, there was an increase in the enrollment in this type of institution; and noted experts in education were recommending that students acquire a liberal arts education. The assessment of internal strengths indicated that the new mission could be pursued in light of sufficient liberal arts curricular offerings in basic academic areas; talent and diversity in the faculty; classroom, laboratory, and residence hall space; financial reserves; library resources; and faculty/staff support. The assessment of internal weaknesses indicated that selected graduate and undergraduate academic programs would need to be strengthened, and others phased out; selected classrooms and laboratories would need to be modified; selected academic programs would need to be initiated; faculty would need to be given opportunities for retraining; and university funds would have to be reallocated. When all of the positive and negative internal factors and the external factors were assessed collectively, this portion of the new institutional mission statement was enthusiastically accepted by the faculty and staff. At this point, the meaning of the mission had to be defined more clearly in terms of institutional goals; and, following this, the operational plan for achieving the mission had to be developed and implemented in the individual departments and programs of the institution.

This example is but a brief sketch of the assessment and strategic planning needed to develop a small portion of a mission statement for an institution. A large amount of other data would have to be collected and a tremendous number of decisions would have to be made in order to develop a new mission statement.

Staffing and timing are both critical components in conducting the research needed to support the strategic planning and the development of an institutional mission statement. The rule of thumb for staffing and participation is to have broad-based involvement and representation of both faculty and administrators. If a subcommittee working structure is used, then both faculty and administrators should be on each subcommittee. Also, faculty and administrators should both be used to chair subcommittees. Some institutions may also choose to involve students and staff in this process. Broad-based involvement and representation help to ensure that the end product (the mission statement) will represent individuals at all levels within the institution and that these individuals (and hopefully those whom they represent) will assume ownership and identification with the mission statement if they participated in its development.

A great deal of time is required to develop a valid institutional mission statement. Initially, decisions have to be made regarding what data and information have to be gathered. Once the data and information have been gathered, these have to be reviewed and analyzed by the committee before a draft of the mission statement can be developed. It also takes a great deal of discussion and writing to develop what the committee considers to be the appropriate wording of the mission statement. Finally, getting approval of the document by the governing body of the institution, faculty, and administration will usually require the development of several revisions of the mission statement before it is acceptable to all of these groups. At least 6 months are required to develop, write, and gain an acceptance of an institutional mission statement. Many institutions spend an entire academic year in the development of this document. And one of the greatest challenges faced during this period of public review is retaining sufficient substance to provide a clear sense of institutional direction, rather than appeasing all aspects of the institution with a mission statement that is acceptable to all because it lacks any substance.

Obviously, there are many approaches that can be used to develop a new mission statement. Whatever an institution's approach, it is important to remember that the institutional mission statement forms the blueprint for identification of institutional goals and intended departmental and program statements of outcomes and objectives. This document, the institutional mission statement, also provides the ultimate basis for the evaluation of institutional effectiveness.

Developing Institutional Goals

The institutional mission statement should be worded so that persons reading it have no doubt as to the overall direction and orientation of the institution. However, this document does not articulate the mission of the institution at a level of detail that will support the development of a set of departmental/program priorities for action.

If we return to the blueprint analogy, the mission statement is analogous to the initial plot-plan an architect develops for a new university. An initial plot-plan lays out which buildings and roads will be in which location without describing in great detail the internal structure of each of the buildings. Just as an architect develops plans that describe each building in detail, the faculty and administration must add more specificity to the mission statement. As the architect develops a detailed plan that a builder uses to construct the buildings, the faculty and administration must add detail to their mission statement so that operational plans in the institution's departments/programs can be developed.

Initially, an architect develops an overall plan for a building, and later he or she develops the many detailed drawings that are needed by the craftsmen who will build the building. The development of institutional goals to accompany a mission statement is analogous to the development of the overall plan for the building from an initial plot-plan. Institutional goals remain relatively general in nature, and they articulate the direction given to key concepts within the institution that identify what is to be accomplished. As a chief architect would give an initial or rough plan for a building to one of his or her colleagues who is going to develop the final plan, institutional goals should be developed and published within an institution to give direction to personnel at all levels within the institution as they develop operational plans and intended outcomes or objectives, thus determining how institutional goals will be accomplished.

Who should develop the institutional goals? The personnel mix required to develop these goals is identical to that needed to develop the institutional mission. Broad-based involvement of faculty and administrators (and possibly students and staff) is a requirement. It is critical that each of these groups agrees to the validity of the goals, believes these goals represent both its own best interests and those of the institution as a whole, and accepts the need to work toward accomplishment of the goals. Without broad-based involvement and acceptance of the institutional mission and goals, the results of strategic planning will go unused, the institution will not grow and develop, and there will be no way to assess institutional effectiveness.

A great deal of data are gathered and used in the process of developing the mission statement. Along with the analysis of the data, there will be debate as to the relevance and meaning of the data to the institution. Because the goals form a document that is one level of specificity greater than the mission statement, all of the information gathered in the earlier endeavor will apply to the development of the goals. In the development of the mission statement, some of the questions asked are as follows:

Should we do _____ ?

Can we move in "that" direction?

Are we capable of doing _____ ?

What will be the consequences of _____ ?

What implications does this have for _____ ?

Can we add _____ ?

What will be the effect of _____ ?

The questions asked in developing the institution's goals are very different from these. Because the decision to move the institution in a particular direction(s) has already been made during development of the mission statement, the questions change from Should we? to How much?. Some of the questions asked are the following:

How much should we increase by _____ [date]?

What administrative or academic organization will best accomplish _____ ?

What level of funding will be required to reach _____ by _____ [date]?

What level of enrollment (or staffing) must we reach in order to ?

What changes in the physical plant must be made by _____ [date] in order to _____ ?

The answers to these and other similar questions will result in the development of a valid set of goals for an institution.

There are several parameters that must be understood—and set— before an institution can begin to develop its institutional goals. The questions to be asked are

1. What structure will be used in organizing and sequencing the goals?
2. What time frame(s) and level of specificity will be used in the writing of the goals?
3. What level of the operation of the institution will warrant development of goals?

Each of these questions should be answered in detail before goals are written.

Although goals are typically written one at a time, writers must have thought their way through some structure before they begin. Without a structure, it is easy to overlook important concepts and difficult to arrange the goals for presentation once they have been developed. The sample goals in Appendix A (see page 167) follow a modification of the overall administrative organization of Our University. In this document, there are goals for each of the major administrative subdivisions of the institution. For the most part, the goals for each administrative subdivision are ones that can be pursued more or less independently by the staff in that subdivision. Those goals that seem to cut across or require the joint effort of two or more administrative subdivisions appear in the first section of this statement. Note that because all of the subdivisions work to support the academic, research, and service missions of the institution, goals are developed for all of the administrative subdivisions. This means that all of these subdivisions should participate in institutional effectiveness assessment.

Whenever mission or goals statements are developed at an institution, they are built on selected assumptions that are relevant at the time the goals statements are developed. Because the purpose of this entire endeavor is to assess institutional effectiveness, by all means include assumptions with your goals. It is amazing how quickly institutions forget (or selectively modify) their original assumptions. If the assumptions are not recorded, it will be impossible to assess institutional effectiveness validly in the future.

Well-written institutional goals contain two major ingredients. First, they include a description of some well-defined or measurable/accessible end result. Examples of these types of statements include the following:

Enrollment will reach _____ .

Admissions will achieve an acceptance rate of _____ .

Five new academic programs will _____ .

The development office will reach an alumni-giving rate of _____ .

Student services will have programs that will _____ .

The library will have holdings of _____ .

Financial aid will reach a support rate of _____ .

Note that some of the goals specify or state that a specific number, percentage, or rate be reached, whereas others state that something will be accomplished. Both are equally important and valid goals. Note also that the concepts stated in these goals are very broad and inclusive.

If these statements are written very specifically or narrowly, then they become departmental/program objectives or outcomes, not goals. Keep in mind that the purpose of developing the mission and goals statements is to develop documents which, when distributed on campus, can give others direction and assistance as they develop the outcomes and objectives that they will operationalize. If the goals become too specific, they infringe upon the work and professional responsibility of others. Also, if goals statements are written too specifically, then an inordinately large number of them must be developed. From an assessment point of view, an excessive number of goals create personnel, time, and cost problems.

The second ingredient in a goals statement is the time frame. In the examples of goals given earlier, the end result was stated, but the reader was never told when it would occur. There was no way of telling whether it would occur next semester, next year, or in five years. It is important that the time required to achieve the intended action be stated as a part of the goal. Just as some changes within an institution are easier to make than others, it takes more time to achieve one goal than another. Changes in academic programs sometimes take as much as 4 years, major changes in budget allocations can usually be made in 2 years, changes in admissions ratios can be made in 1 year, and changes in institutional investment strategies can be made in several months. Obviously, the time frame used in a goal statement must fit the aspect of the institution to which it applies. It is even possible to use longitudinal time frames in developing goals. For example, a reasonable goal of this type might be as follows: The student retention/graduation rate will increase by 1% in each of the next 5 years and reach 70% by 19___. There are many options open to the creative persons or groups who develop mission and goals statements.

What aspects or subdivisions of an institution warrant the development of institutional goals? The answer is that since no one major aspect or subdivision of the institution is independent of the others, then all warrant the development of goals. However, when an institution chooses to evaluate and change its mission, there tend to be some aspects or subdivisions that become more critical than others. If, for example, an institution chose to pursue academic excellence, then the quality of entering students, the quality of the faculty, the curriculum, and finances needed to support the endeavor would become key concepts of the plan for change. If, in turn, these were the key concepts, then admissions, faculty recruiting, faculty development, curriculum council, financial aid, the development office, budget allocations, and so forth would become the key institutional operations within the plan for change. Assuming that this string of logic is valid and that the list of key concepts and institutional operations is complete, then the Mission and Goals Committee should pay special attention to developing the institutional goals to accompany what they consider to be the key to the plan for change. This approach will focus the attention of the institution on the key concepts and help avoid the development of an excessive number of goals. It is critical that all of the key concepts in the planned change be covered by a goal, but it is just as important that an institution not write so many goals that it is overburdened by their sheer number. Balance and inclusiveness are critical when it comes to developing the proper types and number of institutional goals.

Although the mission statement is typically one to three pages in length, the institutional goals statement is from five to ten pages in length. Larger, complex institutions tend to have longer institutional goals statements than smaller institutions. At most institutions it takes far less time to develop the institutional goals statement than it does to gather data, do the strategic planning, and develop the mission statement. It is conceivable that the goals statement can be developed in as little as 3 months. As with the mission statement, approval for the institutional goals statement should be obtained from the governing board of the institution, the faculty, and the administration.

Summary

When the institutional mission and goals statements are completed, they are the documents that will give direction for operational planning within all levels of the institution and, in turn, will give direction to the majority of the activities and efforts within the institution. These two documents comprise the Expanded Statement of Institutional Purpose, which, in conjunction with the more operational plans of the departments/programs, acts as the evaluation blueprint in assessing institutional effectiveness.

References: Cited and Recommended

Caruthers, J. K., & Lott, G. B. (1981). *Mission review: Foundation for strategic planning*. Boulder, CO: National Center for Higher Education Management Systems.

Chaffee, E. E. (1985). The concept of strategy: From business to higher education. *Annual Handbook of Higher Education, 1,* 133–172.

Cope, R. (1981). *Strategic planning, management and decision making*. American Association for Higher Education.

Dutton, J. L., Fahey, L., & Narayanan, V. K. (1983). Toward understanding strategic issue diagnosis. *Strategic Management Journal, 4,* 307–323.

Ewell, P. T. (Ed.). (1985). *Assessing educational outcomes*. New Directions in Institutional Research, no. 47. San Francisco: Jossey-Bass.

Keller, G. (1983). *Academic strategy: The management revolution in American higher education*. Baltimore, MD: Johns Hopkins University Press.
Kotler, P., & Murphy, P. E. (1981). Strategic planning for higher education. *Journal of Higher Education, 52*, 470–489.
Shirley, R. C. (1982). Limiting the scope of strategy: A decision based approach. *Academy of Management Review, 7*(2), 262–268.
Shirley, R. C. (1983). Identifying the levels of strategy for a college or university. *Long Range Planning, 16*(3), 92–98.

Attitudinal Surveys in Institutional Effectiveness

Gale Bridger

> O wad some Pow'r the giftie gie us
> To see oursels as ithers see us!
> It wad frae mony a blunder free us,
> And foolish notion.

> —*Robert Burns*, "To a Louse"

Surveys designed to measure the attitudes of an institution's various constituents provide important insights into the way others perceive the institution—its purpose, programs, and performance. These attitudinal surveys take many forms, address a range of publics, and generate a wealth of information to be ploughed back into the planning/evaluative process. If not carefully selected, administered, and utilized, they may also simply generate reams of paper which lie fallow on the shelf in some institutional researcher's office. This resource section includes

1. A review of the survey instruments available commercially;
2. A consideration of the usefulness of contracted services;
3. An examination of the value of instruments developed in-house.

Pertinent to this discussion are these topics:

1. The identification of the kinds of information that can be acquired most effectively with survey techniques

2. The constituent groups who may best provide the information sought
3. The campus groups (central administration, student services, academic departments, e.g.) that may benefit from the information so generated

Finally, with these points of selection and application covered, the section contains some practical steps for conducting the surveys and disseminating the information for its effective use.

Commercially Available Surveys

The following agencies offer a full range of survey services that have been subjected to careful testing over a number of years to provide valid, reliable attitudinal data from several population groups:

1. The American College Testing Program (ACT) offers the ACT Evaluation/Survey Service (ESS).
2. The College Board in cosponsorship with the National Center for Higher Education Management Systems (NCHEMS) has available the Student Outcomes Information Service (SOIS).
3. Educational Testing Service offers a family of instruments including Institutional Goals Inventory (IGI), Institutional Functioning Inventory (IFI), Student Reactions to College (SRC), and Program Self-Assessment Service (PSAS).
4. A fourth survey, the oldest and perhaps most widely known, targets one population only and is included here although it is not in the truest sense commercial. The Cooperative Institutional Research Program (CIRP) of the University of California, Los Angeles, and the American Council on Education maintains longitudinal data on American higher education and conducts annually the CIRP survey of entering freshmen.

American College Testing Program

The American College Testing Program Evaluation/Survey Service (ACT/ESS) now offers 12 survey instruments for use by colleges and universities. Each is an optical-scan instrument containing two or four pages of questions designed to permit a general evaluation of an institution's programs and services. Local personnel are afforded the option of designing 20 to 30 additional questions for inclusion in each survey. ACT also offers a catalog of additional items, which institutions may select from in lieu of writing their own questions. In addition, each instrument provides space for the participant to write comments or suggestions. Since 1979, over a million ESS instruments have been administered at more than 750 institutions. This extensive use of the ACT materials has made possible normative data for comparative studies as well as an opportunity for longitudinal studies within institutions. A brief description of each instrument follows.

The College Student Needs Assessment Survey is used to explore the educational and personal needs of enrolled college students and examine their career and life goals. This four-page questionnaire is comprised of five sections:

1. Background information—provides basic demographic data and information for subgroup selection for analysis of the student's responses
2. Career and life goals—gathers information on college major, occupational choice, and relative importance of various goals (both career and personal)
3. Educational and personal needs—asks the student to indicate need for a "lot of help" to "no help" in the areas of career development, educational planning, intellectual skills development, and life skills development
4. (and 5.) Additional questions, comments, and suggestions

The Adult Learner Needs Assessment Survey can be used to examine the education-related needs of adult learners and includes in its four pages items relating to the following:

1. Background—particularly as related to previous educational experience, family, and employment
2. Educational plans and preferences—with emphasis on the special needs of the adult, such as scheduling, location, and format of classes
3. Personal and educational needs—includes life skills development, educational planning, and association with others
4. Additional questions, comments, and suggestions

The Alumni Survey is useful in ascertaining the impact of the institution on its graduates. Four-page surveys are available for two-year and four-year institutions and provide information in the following sections:

1. Background information—tailored to the two-year or four-year graduate
2. Continuing education—provides extensive information on formal education since graduation/departure
3. Educational/college experiences—gauges the alumnus's perception of the value and impact of his or her education in areas such as quality of life, skills development, and independent living
4. Employment history—provides valuable information for alumni and placement offices as well as for various academic program planners
5. (and 6.–7.) Additional questions, mailing addresses, and comments and suggestions—provide additional information that may be useful locally

The Entering Student Survey, a four-page form consisting of five sections, is used to obtain information on the entering student's background, interests, and perception of the institution.

1. Background information
2. Educational plans and preferences—Unlike in the ACT Profile, responses come only from entering college freshmen, not from people in their junior year in high school.
3. College impressions—asks the student to rate the importance of various items in his or her decision to attend the school. The student also is asked to indicate agreement or disagreement with various descriptors providing a perception of the institution as held by entering students.
4. (and 5.) Additional questions, comments, and suggestions

The Student Opinion Survey, with two-year and four-year forms, is used to examine the perception held by enrolled, continuing students of their college's services and environment. The two-year form also includes items to explore the student's reasons for selecting the college and his or her overall impression of the school.

1. Background information
2. Use of and level of satisfaction with various campus services and programs
3. Level of satisfaction with the college environment in the following areas: academic, admissions, rules and regulations, facilities, registration, and general
4. Additional questions, comments, and suggestions

The Survey of Academic Advising is used to obtain information regarding student impressions of academic advising services. The four-page form includes the following:

1. Background information
2. Advising information—including frequency of advisor-and-advisee contacts and the period of time the student has been assigned to the current advisor
3. Academic advising needs—in which the student identifies topics discussed with the advisor and expresses his or her level of satisfaction with the advisor's assistance
4. (and 5.) Additional questions, comments, and suggestions

The Survey of Current Activities and Plans is designed for applicants to the institution who chose *not* to enroll. The survey requests the following:

1. Background information
2. Impressions of the college
3. Educational plans and activities
4. Employment plans
5. Additional questions, comments, and suggestions

The Survey of Postsecondary Plans is used with high school students to identify their occupational and educational plans after high school graduation. This survey also asks for impressions held by the student of the particular institution conducting the survey and offers space for additional questions and for comments and suggestions. Information from the first part of this survey is not unlike that in the ACT Profile.

The Withdrawing/Nonreturning Student Survey is produced in both a two-page (short form) and four-page format. In both the student who chooses to leave college before completing a degree is asked to provide background information and to indicate reasons for leaving. These reasons are grouped in the following categories:

1. Personal (health, moving, marriage, social, etc.)
2. Academic (suspension, instructional quality, not challenged, etc.)
3. Institutional (scheduling problems, inadequate advising, programs or facilities, etc.)
4. Financial (availability of work or financial aid)
5. Employment (conflict between work and school, etc.)

Both forms also provide space for comments and suggestions. The long form, in addition, asks for the student to rate his or her satisfaction with various institutional services and characteristics.

ACT offers a variety of flexible services, and institutions may elect simply to purchase one or more of the survey instruments or to contract for a full range of mailing, scoring and reporting services.

Student Outcomes Information Service

The Student Outcomes Information Service (SOIS), cosponsored by the College Board and the National Center for Higher Education Management Systems, is in many respects like the ACT/ESS. The questionnaires focus on six different points during and after college:

1. Entering student
2. Continuing student
3. Program completer and graduating student
4. Former student
5. Recent alumnus
6. Three- to five-year follow-up

The questionnaires, offered in formats for both two-year and four-year institutions, provide background demographics; survey educational experiences, plans, and goals; identify need for, use of, and satisfaction with institutional services; and give perceptions and impressions of the institution as held by the various survey populations.

Perhaps the most significant difference between the SOIS and ACT families of surveys is the coordinated, research-oriented approach of the SOIS which is supported by a carefully written handbook, *Student Outcomes Questionnaires: An Implementation Handbook* (2nd edition, 1983), by Peter T. Ewell.

Ewell takes the novice practitioner through the process step by step and carefully points out tricks and essential steps to help guarantee successful, usable survey results. As with ACT, data processing and questionnaire analyses are available. Annual summaries of information from participating institutions are also made available.

Educational Testing Service

The Educational Testing Service (ETS) College and University Programs offer a different array of survey instruments focusing primarily on program planning and evaluation. The following components of the Institutional Research Program for Higher Education (IRPHE) are available from ETS:

1. Institutional Goals Inventory (IGI)
2. Community College Goals Inventory (CCGI)
3. Small College Goals Inventory (SCGI)
4. Program Self-Assessment Service (PSAS)
5. Graduate Program Self-Assessment Service (GPSA)
6. Student Reactions to College (SRC)
7. Institutional Functioning Inventory (IFI)
8. Student Instructional Report (SIR)

The goals inventories (IGI, CCGI, and SCGI) differ in content and focus in addressing the concerns of the three different types of institutions (i.e., university or large college, community college, and small college). In format, however, they are alike—each has 90 statements of possible institutional goals, and participants are asked to indicate their opinions of the importance of each statement in terms of both what exists and what they would *like to see exist*, providing a future orientation as well as a look at the present. The inventory is appropriate for use by students, faculty, and administrators, thus offering the opportunity to gain perceptions of the institution's goals and purpose. A Canadian IGI in both French and English and a Spanish/English IGI are available, as is a Canadian CCGI in English only.

The Program Self-Assessment Service (PSAS) consists of a set of questionnaires that address areas such as curriculum, program purposes, departmental procedures, faculty activity, student accomplishment, and the general environment for work and learning. The PSAS assumes that the perceptions and assessment of those most directly involved with any department or program can contribute to an improved quality and functioning of the area surveyed. Thus, the service offers three assessment questionnaires: for faculty, students who major in the department or program, and recent graduates of the program. Responses provide a profile of the targeted program or department and can assist in the program review process by identifying areas of strength and those areas that need attention.

The Graduate Program Self-Assessment Service (GPSAS) is the parent of the previously described PSAS. GPSA is cosponsored by the Graduate Record Examination Board and the Council of Graduate Schools in the United States. Instruments have been developed for both master's and doctoral level programs and address the parallel constituent groups identified in the PSAS discussion, i.e., students enrolled in the program, faculty, and recent graduates. Survey questions provide information on 16 areas of program characteristics including environment for learning, scholarly excellence, teaching quality, faculty concern for students, curriculum, departmental procedures, resources (such as library and laboratories), faculty work environment, student accomplishments, and others.

The Student Reactions to College (SRC) survey is used to solicit opinions from enrolled students about their college experience: instruction, counseling, out-of-class activities, administrative affairs, and so forth. The 150-item questionnaire is grouped into 19 areas of interest and provides information about the needs and concerns of students. There are separate forms for community colleges (SRC–2) and for four-year colleges and universities (SRC–4).

The Institutional Functioning Inventory (IFI) is helpful to faculty, students, and administrators who wish to assess administrative policies, teaching practices, and academic and extracurricular programs. The questionnaire consists of 132 items; students surveyed respond only to items 1 through 72. The IFI grew out of a study of institutional vitality supported by the Kettering Foundation; and comparative data are available for public universities, four-year state colleges, private liberal arts colleges, community colleges, and private junior colleges.

The Student Instructional Report (SIR) is a brief, objective questionnaire that helps instructors gain information about students' reactions to their courses. The questionnaire offers students the opportunity to comment anonymously on their courses and instruction. Six factors are covered:

1. Course organization and planning
2. Faculty–student interaction
3. Communication
4. Course difficulty and work load
5. Textbooks and readings
6. Tests and/or examinations

The SIR is not intended to replace regular student–faculty communication. It does provide an additional means by which instructors may examine their teaching performance.

Extensive comparative data are available through ETS based on SIR administrations in the United States and Canada. The questionnaire is available in Spanish and in a Canadian version in both French and English.

All of the ETS instruments offer space for optional local items, and like ACT and College Board/NCHEMS, the services of basic data processing and reporting are available. Special services and professional assistance may be negotiated as well.

Cooperative Institutional Research Program

The Student Information Form (SIF) used in the Cooperative Institutional Research Program (CIRP) contains standard biographic and demographic data-gathering items which have been regularly included for each entering freshman class. It also contains research-oriented attitudinal questions which are modified from time to time. The SIF includes a wide-ranging set of questions, including items dealing with students' personal habits, reasons for attending college, political views, and others. The report, generated by the optical-scanned responses and provided to the institution, gives responses in percentages for the institution and comparative data for all institutions in the participant institution's category.

Contracted Services

Most management consultant services and marketing consultants are capable of developing and conducting surveys of the public to determine perceptions about a given institution's reputation, purposes, and programs. A number of agencies now market themselves primarily to the higher education community. Because these are organizations in a highly competitive market, individual groups will not be identified here. However, there are some advantages to contracting for survey services:

1. The contract is usually for a turnkey process (i.e., it includes tailoring the survey to the specific needs of the client, gathering and processing the data, and presenting and interpreting the results to appropriate groups).
2. The contractual process may be regarded more favorably by those surveyed because it is individualized and carries the identity of the contracting institution.
3. The contractor may provide on-site consultants who may lend added credibility to the process and the findings through discussion with others.

An excellent example of the best contractual arrangements is that offered by NCHEMS through its Institutional Performance Survey

(IPS). The focus of the IPS is comprehensive measurement of the institution through questions regarding effectiveness, leadership and decision styles, and institutional culture and environment. Although the instrument used is standard, the total survey-and-consultant process is tailored to the needs of the campus. Because the survey is standard, the total cost is significantly lower than what could be anticipated from an individually designed survey.

Several disadvantages of contracted services are as follows:

1. An institution may expect the contract cost to run as high as $30,000 to $40,000.
2. The resultant data will not have the benefits of comparability to normative data or summary data from other institutions of the same level or type.
3. The time required for the full development of such services may be counterproductive.

These disadvantages may be negated when the institution's needs are determined to be met best by a specially designed survey.

Frequently, for example, institutions are interested in gaining through telephone sampling or similar marketing techniques reputational kinds of information or community needs assessment data. Such services contracted by local sampling and marketing agencies may be quite successful and not unduly expensive. This approach should, in fact, be selected if (a) available commercial instruments do not meet the institution's identified need, (b) the expertise of labor force is not available in-house, or (c) the contracted arrangement can provide the data required in a cost-effective and timely manner.

Surveys Developed In-house

Locally developed in-house survey instruments take time and expertise to develop. However, most campuses will have individuals in their social science or education departments or in their offices of institutional research who have knowledge of the methodology necessary to develop these surveys. And, of course, they are likely to be cheaper. H. R. Kells, in *Self-Study Processes* (1980), reminds us that "a poorly designed instrument, used at the wrong moment with an unreceptive audience, will yield little or no useful information and it may damage the sense of community and morale at the institution involved" (p. 69). On the other hand, recognizing and using local expertise to produce a well-developed survey and provide prompt analysis and dissemination of results may be the most effective way to gain a sense of ownership for the entire assessment/evaluation process.

Northeast Missouri State University, which has one of the three foremost models for institutional effectiveness programs, designed a set of survey instruments early in its assessment plan development. One of the interesting secondary benefits of these locally designed surveys is the frequent, prominent use of the institution's name on the survey forms.

Rhode Island College has administered its own entering student questionnaire (still in provisional form) to provide data for individualized learning plans for its students. Special needs and goals call for special instruments.

For those who determine that in-house surveys will serve them best, a look at the content of commercial surveys reviewed earlier in this section may give the developer a head start on the general areas to include. Particularly important are the following:

1. Demographic data so that subgroups of data may be examined
2. An opportunity for comments
3. A thank you to improve response rate

Characteristics of Survey Information

Survey information falls into two categories: (a) factual, demographic data and (b) opinions or perceptions. A caution about each category is in order here. First, some demographic data are perhaps verifiable by checking other sources of, for example, student information. However, that process would be time-consuming and certainly not generally needed. The caution here is simply that responses to survey items may not be absolutely accurate. A participant may subtract or add years to his or her age; an alumnus may exaggerate income. Still, most respondents tend to answer honestly and accurately, and for the purposes of the survey the information has value.

A more significant caution regards the second category—opinions or perceptions. The institution's leadership must be certain to recognize that these results are just that—perceptions, not necessarily reality or fact. They may tell us a great deal about how we are viewed by others or by ourselves, but these must be taken alongside other kinds of data (quantitative, measurable information) to have a complete picture of the institution, its strengths and its shortcomings.

Survey Populations

By referring to the various surveys developed by the testing agencies and reviewed on the first pages of this section, we may immediately identify some of the survey populations whose opinions and perceptions we value. These include students, faculty, and alumni, and subgroups of those (e.g., entering students, nonreturning students, recent alumni, perhaps even tenured faculty). Other survey populations on campus might be administrators and nonteaching staff.

The general population in the institution's service area is an appropriate survey population for reputational-type surveys. Perhaps employers of the institution's graduates are another valuable survey group. Any group of individuals who uses or may use the institution's service or in some other way has contact with and knowledge of the institution is an appropriate survey population, depending on the kind of information sought.

The first question an institution may ask when considering attitudinal surveys is, What do we want to know? The second question is, Who can tell us best? Thus are populations chosen. Once chosen, good research practices must be followed in sampling the populations. Certainly, wherever possible, surveying the total group is helpful. (For example, faculty, administrators, or nonreturning students may be surveyed as a total group.)

Information Users

With surveys selected and information gathered from populations defined, let us not relegate the results to a shelf somewhere. Who will use the information? Each campus will have its own individualized list, but perhaps these suggested users may help in planning meetings for dissemination of information.

Information/Perceptions	*Users*
Student Services	Registrar
	Student Affairs Officers
	Counselors
	Activities Director
	Student Government Association
	Financial Aid Officer

Academic Programs	Academic Vice President
	Academic Deans
	Department Chairs
	Curriculum Committees
	Faculty
Facilities	Central Administration
	Physical Plant Director
	Building Managers
	Librarian
	Athletics/Intramural
	Sports Director
Administration	President
	Administrative Staff
	Vice Presidents

For most efficient use of the results, a comparison of a group's intended attitudinal outcomes or objectives with related data generated through survey processes will bring these relationships into focus. Groups may then proceed with action plans to test further the effectiveness of their programs and services or to revise those offerings. A sharply honed presentation related specifically to the user group in that group's language and frame of reference, in other words, is essential.

Design for Survey Implementation and Dissemination of Results

The implementation of a program of attitudinal surveys should be undertaken systematically with clear results in mind. Representatives from each of the potential user groups should be involved in the process, participating in the identification of survey populations and of kinds of information desired. The following sequence of activities should occur. The subpoints are given as examples and should trigger additional items specific to the institution's needs.

1. Identification of intended results for the survey activity, for example:
    a. To acquire additional personal and demographic information about various student, alumni, and other population groups
    b. To gain information for program improvement

    c. To obtain perceptions of institutional quality

    d. To inform external publics of the institution's characteristics

2. Selection of appropriate instruments, considering, for example:

    a. Available financial resources

    b. In-house expertise and data processing support

    c. Content of commercially available instruments

    d. Feasibility of longitudinal use

3. Establishment of a time schedule for administration:

    a. Entering students—each orientation period

    b. Continuing students—every third year? alternate years?

    c. Exiting/noncontinuing students—as part of exiting process

    d. Graduating seniors—as a part of the diploma application, graduation checkout, or similar activity

    e. Recent alumni—every year within 6 months of graduation

    f. Alumni follow-up—each year for graduates 5 years out or, perhaps, every other year or every third year for classes 3 to 5 years out

    g. Program-related questionnaire—at the time of program review, or, perhaps, every 5 years

    h. External publics—at 5- to 10-year intervals, particularly at times of mission review or as needed to identify new constituencies or new programs

4. Collection and interpretation of data, considering, for example:

    a. Contractual arrangements for mailing, processing, tabulating, and summarizing data

    b. Assignment of personnel and allocation of release time for these activities

    c. Establishment of types of reporting desired (i.e., means, percentages, comparisons, simple frequencies) by subgroups or aggregated only

5. Dissemination of information:

    a. Identification of key user groups

    b. Partitioning of data into manageable segments (not everything to everybody at one time)

    c. Scheduling of small-group sessions for presentation and interpretation of data

6. Follow-up sessions to review:

    a. Usefulness of information as catalyst for change or in reaffirmation of status quo, or for initiation of new programs and services

    b. Need for additional data

c. Need for instrument redesign or continued use

d. Longitudinal implementation of survey cycle

As one examines the preceding outline, a number of additional questions, items for inclusion, or cautions will come to mind. The cross fertilization of ideas and needs that surfaces in discussions with key user representatives as they deal with these additional items may be as valuable to the health of the institution as the resultant survey data.

Some key elements for that group to keep in mind to help ensure success for the program follow.

1. Avoid overcontact with survey populations. It is important that the same community leader, alumnus, or, for that matter, continuing students not be asked at too frequent (1 year or less) intervals to participate in survey activities. The key to avoiding this problem is to establish a central office which, at the least, serves as a clearinghouse for all such activity and, at the most, conducts the gathering and dissemination of all such data. The oversurveying of populations is not cost-effective, gives fragmented information, and may well alienate the survey participant, thus yielding less dependable data and creating public relations problems for the institution. Alumni surveys are an easy prey to this problem. For example, the Placement Office conducts a career satisfaction survey, the Development Office asks many of the same questions in a survey designed to identify potential donors, and the graduate's academic department asks these questions to determine achievement of programmatic goals. One survey, centrally coordinated with participation by all these users in its development and in planning for dissemination of results, will develop much more positive relationships between the institution and its alumni.

2. Establish a plan for multiple contacts for mail surveys to increase response rate.

    a. A letter from the CEO or other key officer (the student's dean, perhaps, in the case of program-related surveys) explaining the need for the information and appealing to the person's loyalties as a member of the institutional community will convey the importance of the survey and place it in a positive light.

    b. Inclusion of a postage-paid return envelope is advisable, as is the mailing of surveys at forwarding-address-requested level of postage rather than at a lower rate.

c. A follow-up post-card reminder is helpful. Of even greater effect is a personal phone call which, in some cases, may be linked to calls for other purposes: recruitment calls to applicants, calls encouraging continuing students to pre-register, or fund drive calls to alumni and community, for example.

d. Some institutions have even included a dime or, perhaps, a pencil or pen with the school's name stamped on it or a small note pad. These add little to the cost and may be an additional enticement to the person being surveyed.

3. Be certain if work is being done in-house that the time, personnel, and facilities are adequate to the task. If these requirements are not met, the project is very likely to bog down. Appropriate follow-up cannot occur if data are not processed in a timely fashion, and any positive effect of the earlier activities is quickly lost if user groups cannot see the results of their earlier efforts and if the public surveyed sees no evidence of use of the results. It is sometimes much more cost-effective and profitable to the institution to forego some individualized information needs to take advantage of the efficiency of basic services offered by the various testing services.

4. Select segmented elements of data for presentation over a continuing period of time and be certain to follow up on their use. Peter Ewell, in *Assessment, Accountability, and Improvement: Managing the Contradiction* (1987), made this point emphatically: *"Don't show everything at once."* Ewell's point is to guarantee that the institution will continue to have new information to report and to demonstrate ongoing commitment. Accountability to our external constituencies may require this kind of juggling of information. Internal accountability, however, needs this segmentation of information for a different purpose: a user may focus on narrower areas for improvement and change, and that concentration of effort is more likely to result in a stronger institution than are attempts to address all areas simultaneously.

Summary

Patricia Hutchings, in *Six Stories: Implementing Successful Assessment* (1987), says, "In some ways the important point may be less *what* one does than the need to do *something*. Yes, everything will be imperfect, it's better on paper." Certainly, a plan for attitudinal surveys is a way to "do something" and offer constructive, useful results in the early stages of an assessment process.

The institution that takes the steps necessary to implement attitudinal surveys will indeed see itself as others see it, and it will, if the information is carefully used, free itself from many a blunder and foolish notion.

References: Cited and Recommended

The ACT evaluation/survey service, Specimen set [Instruments]. Iowa City, IA: American College Testing Program.

Assessment Resource Center bibliography. (1987). Knoxville, TN: Assessment Resource Center, University of Tennessee.

Astin, A. W. (1986). *The American freshman: National norms for fall 1986.* Los Angeles, CA: Cooperative Institutional Research Program, University of California.

Cavanaugh, D., & Sollner, P. (1987). The FIPSE value-added grant for Rhode Island College. Unpublished paper presented to the Educational Testing Service Conference on Value-Added Assessment.

Criteria for accreditation: Commission on colleges (Section III). Atlanta, GA: Southern Association of Colleges and Schools, pp. 10–11.

ESS in action. (1987). Iowa City, IA: American College Testing Program.

ETS college and university programs [Brochure]. Princeton, NJ: Educational Testing Service.

Ewell, P. T. (1983). *Student outcomes questionnaires: An implementation handbook* (2nd ed.). Boulder, CO: National Center for Higher Education Management Systems.

Ewell, P. T. (1984). *The self-regulating institution: Information for excellence.* Boulder, CO: National Center for Higher Education Management Systems.

Ewell, P. T. (1987). *Assessment, accountability and improvement: Managing the contradiction.* Washington, DC: American Association for Higher Education Assessment Forum.

Hutchings, P. (1987). *Six stories: Implementing successful assessment.* Washington, DC: American Association for Higher Education Assessment Forum.

Institutional performance survey [Instrument]. Boulder, CO: National Center for Higher Education Management Systems.

Kells, H. R. (1980). *Self-study processes: A guide for postsecondary institutions.* Washington, DC: American Council on Education.

Lenning, O. T. (1980). *Retention and attrition: Evidence for action and research.* Boulder, CO: National Center for Higher Education Management Systems.

McClain, C. J. (1987, Winter). Assessment produces degrees with integrity. *Educational Record,* pp. 47–52.

Resource manual on institutional effectiveness. (1987). Atlanta, GA: Commission on Colleges of the Southern Association of Colleges and Schools.

Student-outcomes questionnaires [Instruments]. Boulder, CO: National Center for Higher Education Management Systems.

Cognitive Assessment Instruments: Availability and Utilization

Marsha V. Krotseng

Appropriate Assessment: Which One of the Above?

The current "ubiquity of tests has led some academics who know little about assessment to think the term *means* testing"—and testing alone (Marchese, 1987, p. 6). In fact, number 2 pencils and op-scan computer forms comprise just one (albeit highly visible) element of the process—the act of *cognitive assessment*. Until recently, cognitive assessment meant (as Humpty Dumpty advised Alice) "just what [colleges and universities chose] it to mean—neither more nor less" (Carroll, 1871/1960, p. 269). However, individual institutional strategies for cognitive assessment have culminated in energetic involvement by accrediting agencies and have led to the more systematic scheme represented by the Institutional Effectiveness Paradigm shown as Figure 2 (see p. 30). Rigorous methods and vigorous execution are becoming the order of the day, and the disputations characteristic of medieval universities and their offspring, the American colonial college, have bowed before a host of standardized and locally developed examinations.

The critical question for the 1980s is not whether to saddle this sleek assessment steed, but, rather, how to harness its full potential—without being thrown. As the seasoned rider will analyze a thoroughbred's nature before leaving the gate, university communities can similarly avoid a false start at cognitive assessment by scrutinizing the ever-expanding array of available instruments. Thus, in the following pages the capabilities of several popular cognitive assessment alternatives and their application and practicality in various situations are considered.

However, two primary queries as posed by Halpern (1987a) necessarily precede the selection of an appropriate instrument: "What do you want to know?" and "Why do you want to know it?" (p. 109). "Clear and succinct answers to these questions will [then] provide direction to the secondary questions, 'What should you measure?' and 'How should you measure it?'" (Halpern, p. 109). In the present context, the reason for assessment is readily apparent—to analyze an institution's intended (and actual) educational outcomes. Comprising this path to institutional effectiveness or program improvement are such discrete stepping-stones as the determination of students' academic progress and the use of examinations as "gateways" to upper-division coursework or as benchmarks for budget decisions and accountability (Halpern, 1987b). Once an institution has set forth its Expanded Statement of Institutional Purpose and the supporting departmental/program statements of intended outcomes/objectives, the identification of proper instruments can proceed logically and smoothly. As Harris (1985) concluded, "You can compare your students to [others] nationally on standardized tests without having definite educational goals. . . . But without such goals, you can't be sure the tests reflect your curriculum" (p. 13).

Resnick and Goulden (1987) cited 13 basic methods of assessment of learning originally reported in an American Council on Education survey of 450 college and university presidents and academic vice presidents:

1. College-level skills or minimum competency tests
2. Tests of general knowledge in the humanities and sciences
3. Comprehensive tests in a student's major
4. Tests of critical thinking
5. Tests of quantitative problem solving
6. Tests of oral communication
7. Tests of writing
8. Value-added measures of student gains while in college
9. Mathematics placement tests for entering students
10. English placement tests for entering students
11. Reading placement tests for entering students
12. Placement tests in other skills for entering students
13. Pre- and posttests for remedial courses

Universities and both two-year and four-year colleges commonly employ mathematics, English, and reading placement tests as well as remedial examinations. With the exception of placement tests in other skills, the remaining assessment techniques evidence a high growth potential, particularly at the university level.

General Knowledge: Where Has All the Learning Gone?

Emphasizing breadth across the curriculum rather than in-depth study, tests of general knowledge reveal the students' grasp of basic concepts and skills in the liberal arts (Hartle, 1985). Communication, computation, and critical thinking join elements from the social and natural sciences on both standardized and local instruments intended for this purpose.

Standardized Tests of General Knowledge

College Outcomes Measures Project. In linking specific tests with the preceding ACE enumeration, the American College Testing Program's College Outcomes Measures Project (COMP) stands out as the most popular battery for evaluating students' general knowledge. Administered by over 250 institutions of higher learning, including the University of Tennessee at Knoxville, Northeast Missouri State University, Trenton (New Jersey) State College, Rhode Island College, and King's College (Pennsylvania), the ACT COMP provides three options (Harris, 1985):

1. COMP Composite Examination
2. COMP Objective Test
3. COMP Activity Inventory

The Composite Examination covers the "process" areas of oral and written communication, problem solving, and values clarification together with the "content" areas of "functioning within social institutions," "using science and technology," and "using the arts." Students require approximately 4 hours to complete the entire examination which comprises multiple-choice questions, brief written responses, letter- and memo-writing exercises, and brief oral speeches. With a four-person faculty team, evaluation of the written and oral responses consumes about 50 minutes per student. However, the commitment may be shortened by administering only those portions of this modular examination that are of special concern or relevance (Harris, 1985).

Given such formidable demands on time and energy, it should not be surprising that most institutions (including the University of Tennessee at Knoxville and Rhode Island College) opt for a shorter assessment alternative, the ACT COMP Objective Test. Although this version incorporates the same process and content areas as the Composite Examination, the communication area is not separated into oral and written segments. The Objective Test can be completed in about 2 hours (half the time necessary for the Composite Examination) and requires no faculty evaluation, as it consists entirely of four-option multiple-choice questions (Harris, 1985).

The ACT COMP Activity Inventory serves a slightly different purpose through obtaining "a report from students or alumni of what uses they make of their general education" (e.g., "What actual use would a graduate make of his or her general education literature courses in selecting a novel in a large bookstore?" [Harris, 1985, p. 18]). The Activity Inventory addresses the same three process and content areas as the Composite and Objective Examinations but, unlike its ACT siblings, is not timed. Harris (1985), however, cited research indicating that the inventory generally can be completed within 90 minutes.

Of this ACT COMP trilogy, Harris (1985) prefers the longer Composite Examination because involvement of faculty members in testing and evaluation increases their ownership of the results. Moreover, this option affords faculty "the face-to-face specifics of the students' responses, which encourage them where the students do well and provide them with specific knowledge of deficiencies where the students perform poorly" (Harris, 1985, p. 18). Yet, he has rightfully acknowledged the inordinate amount of student and faculty time encumbered by the Composite Examination—even in a small institution, let alone one with an enrollment in the thousands.

As previously observed, the University of Tennessee at Knoxville has defused this dilemma by turning to the shorter COMP Objective Test. The "largest institutional user of the instrument," the University of Tennessee at Knoxville employs this measure of the outcomes of its general education program "because of the extent of [the test's] coverage, its cost, and the time involved in scoring and interpretation" (Weiner, 1987, p. 13).

After administering the ACT COMP, Trenton State College researchers found a "good (but not outstanding)" correlation of .36 between the total COMP score and grade point average; the correlation between the total COMP score and SAT was slightly higher at .43 (Curry & Hager, 1987). However, Curry and Hager have cautioned that the ACT COMP may not be a very accurate measure of "what is actually being taught" and that each question measures three distinct goals. Thus, the "questions cannot be too specific or too hard (for example, there cannot be any questions on classical music or on calculus) because information would be lost in three different areas" (p. 61). In addition, these authors have argued that some distinctions on the ACT COMP are "somewhat dubious"; because "higher order communication skills branch over into critical thinking and artistic expression," they expected a greater correspondence between students' communication and problem-solving scores (p. 64). Finally, Curry and Hager have contended that the small average difference between the raw scores of freshmen and seniors (8 points) is "not enough to give us much confidence in the results" (p. 62).

Other standardized tests. Trenton State College applied the COMP in conjunction with the experimental Test of General Education (TGE), no longer available from the Educational Testing Service. Before settling on the COMP and TGE alternatives, however, Trenton State College scrutinized its assessment needs in relation to other available standardized tests, among them, the Graduate Record Examination (GRE), the Undergraduate Assessment Program (UAP), the College-Level Examination Program (CLEP), the Miller Analogy Test, and the National Teachers Examination (NTE). Perhaps best known as measures of specialized learning, these instruments also contain a general knowledge component which may prove useful in evaluating institutional effectiveness. Authored by ETS, the GRE discriminates at the upper end of the range and, perhaps, proves most effective as an admissions test. Similarly, the Educational Testing Services's UAP, derived from GRE subject tests, may work most effectively as a selection rather than as an outcomes measurement device (Curry & Hager, 1987). The UAP's three General Education Area Tests in humanities, social science, and natural science are available on loan from ETS. However, as ETS no longer scores the 60-minute examinations, institutions must be prepared to handle this additional dimension themselves. Consequently, the UAP claims no current national norms (Harris, 1985).

Another ETS offering does permit comparison with prevailing national norms: the College-Level Examination Program, or CLEP. Initially designed for high school students desiring college credit, this program provides General Examinations in English composition, mathematics, humanities, natural sciences, and social sciences and history. Although Curry and Hager (1987) found the CLEP somewhat appealing, at three times the length of the TGE, they also felt it "far too long" (p. 61).

Like the GRE, the Miller Analogy Test emerges as a more appropriate tool for admissions than assessment. Another possibility surfaces in the Educational Testing Service's Pre-Professional Skills Test (PPST) of mathematics, reading, and English. Although employed with seeming success at Xavier University in Louisiana, this program's original intent was "to assess readiness for professional practice" (Ewell, 1987, p. 17). Curry and Hager (1987) hailed the general section of the National Teachers Examination as well matched to their institution's particular goals and, hence, as a potentially valuable instrument if area subscores were accessible. At present, results are reported only as English, mathematics, and professional knowledge totals.

Successive administrations of the SAT and ACT entrance examinations form a vital part of the assessment programs at such schools as Northeast Missouri State University and Xavier University. Maricopa Community College District (Arizona) incorporates ACT's ASSET program (representing an "asset for students") in its basic skills entry-level assessment (Weiner, 1987). "Although not generally seen as outcomes assessment, [such] placement testing of students upon entry into college is . . . an excellent example of the formative approach," ideally a step toward instructional improvement (Ewell, 1987, p. 11).

Perhaps the two newest additions to this far-flung family of standardized tests are ACT's recently publicized Collegiate Assessment of Academic Proficiency (CAAP) and the Academic Profile program jointly sponsored by the College Board and ETS. To be offered on a pilot basis during the 1988–89 and 1989–90 academic sessions, the CAAP has been designed to measure general education foundational skills typically strengthened during the first 2 years of college: college-level reading, writing, mathematics, and critical thinking. According to the promotional literature, "CAAP features flexibility," including modular construction, the option for local informational questions, and evaluation of writing skills by means of objective questions and/or sample essays. The pilot tests will be administered in either 1-hour (one content area) or 4-hour (four content areas plus essay) segments.

Similarly, the ETS Academic Profile measures four academic skills (college-level reading, college-level writing, critical thinking, and use of mathematical data) across three contexts (humanities, social sciences, and natural sciences). Pilot tested during 1987 and 1988, the Academic Profile is available in a short (1-hour) form for group assessment or a 3-hour form for group and individual assessment. Results are returned as one total score together with four skills subscores and three content subscores. Like the CAAP, the Academic Profile also provides for an optional 45-minute essay and includes space for a maximum of 50 locally written questions.

Localized General Knowledge Alternatives

With increasing numbers of states and state higher education system offices mandating student assessment, these entities inevitably have fashioned their own alternatives to the familiar standardized route in search of instruments more closely paralleling a particular curriculum. Although many of these state-, system-, and institution-devised substitutes are not strictly local in the sense of being confined to a single place, they are more limited in scope and application and, hence, are referred to in this publication as "local instruments." Such general knowledge examinations are better tailored to local circumstances and needs. By Florida state statute, every community college and state university student must successfully complete all four tests of that state's College Level Academic Skills Project (CLASP). This examination is required for all community college associate degrees as well as for admission to upper-division status in all public universities. Developed by faculty from the Florida community colleges and state universities, CLASP is used to assess skills in both communication (reading, listening, writing, and speaking) and mathematics (algorithms, concepts, generalizations, and problem solving). Although this measure was specifically constructed for Florida institutions of higher learning, the Florida State Department of Education honors legitimate requests from individuals and institutions interested in the CLASP Technical Report and Test Administration Plan (Harris, 1985).

A well-known system-level requirement, the Regents' Testing Program of the University System of Georgia is administered to all rising juniors in the state's community colleges, four-year colleges, and universities. A prerequisite to graduation, the Regents' Program evaluates both reading comprehension and essay construction. The reading portion, a 1-hour test of 60 items, "consists of ten . . . passages, with five to eight questions on each, that test comprehension in terms of vocabulary, literal comprehension, inferential comprehension, and analysis" (Harris, 1985, p. 20). Review of the essay section involves multiple faculty evaluators (who have not taught the students) trained to use a consistent scoring procedure (Harris, 1985).

On the West Coast, the California State University System's Graduation Writing Assessment Requirement (GWAR) demands writing proficiency of all upper-division and graduate students. However, each of the 19 CSU campuses has implemented its own version of this requirement; whereas some campuses designate certain upper-division and graduate-level courses that entail "a large amount of writing," others "allow students to demonstrate proficiency on an actual writing test" (Harris, 1985, p. 20). As in Georgia and New Jersey, multiple faculty evaluations and a consistent grading procedure have proved integral to the process.

Finally, a few hardy institutions like Olivet Nazarene, dissatisfied with the standardized status quo, have assumed the whole burden of developing more satisfactory tests of general education for their students.

Standardized or Local?

Confronted with this assortment of instruments, college faculty members and administrators are well advised to consider their intended educational outcomes together with the strengths and weaknesses of standardized and locally developed examinations before committing to any particular program. Standardized instruments such as the ACT COMP, GRE, and SAT obviously have weathered a number of prior applications and are readily available. More important, Ewell (1987) has described them as

1. Relatively easy to administer;
2. Acceptable in terms of faculty time invested, although costly if used in volume;
3. Generally less open to charges of subjectivity;
4. Nationally normed, allowing comparison across institutions.

On the other hand, standardized examinations suffer major disadvantages in that

1. They may or may not reflect the content of a specific institution's curriculum.
2. The results often are reported as a single performance score (or, at best, four to six subscores), obscuring the laudable as well as the less healthy aspects of the curriculum.
3. Normative comparison scores may be inappropriate for general curriculum evaluation (e.g., GRE norms, compiled from those taking the test, may not be suitable for comparison with scores from an entire graduating class [Ewell, 1987]).

As suggested earlier, the attributes of state- and systemwide examinations alleviate several of these concerns. Specifically, such faculty-developed instruments will be

1. Tailored to the individual curriculum;
2. Available for more detailed analysis of results;
3. Amenable to a variety of formats including essays or task and problem-solving exercises;
4. Perceived as legitimate by faculty since at least key colleagues have played a role in the tests' design (Ewell, 1987).

But, neither are these examinations free of certain drawbacks. According to Ewell (1987), they

1. Reflect only the priorities of a particular institution or system and may, therefore, hold less external credibility;
2. Cannot be compared with results from other institutions or programs outside the system or state;
3. Can be costly to produce, especially in terms of that precious commodity—faculty time;
4. Will not necessarily be well constructed without special on-campus training or expertise.

Specialized Knowledge: A Result of Four Critical Years?

"Comprehensive exams in the major fields or across fields, using essays and oral interrogation and modeled on English university practice, [were] common in American higher education through most of the nineteenth century" (Resnick & Goulden, 1987, p. 80). Indeed, descriptions of senior culminating experiences at Swarthmore and St. Johns have become almost legendary. For the majority of today's institutions, however, standardized examinations in the major field of study afford a more practical alternative for assessing in-depth understanding of a specific subject, commonly referred to as specialized knowledge.

Standardized Tests

According to Harris (1985),

If a department is primarily interested in assessment for program evaluation, it may not need to administer outside tests. Rather, it may be able to use the test results its students and graduates ordinarily provide in their application for graduate or professional education, or for licensure or certification. A post-graduation examination [such as the CPA] . . . will have obvious leverage on the department's faculty. Departments often develop "batting averages" out of such information. (p. 20)

If, instead, circumstances clearly call for outside tests, Harris (1985) has recommended beginning the search for a suitable standardized instrument with the *Test Collection of ETS*. This valuable resource lists equivalency tests, entrance examinations, certification tests, and achievement tests, including for each "an abstract description of the test and its purpose; the components within the overall test that assess particular skills or content; the ages and levels for which the test is [intended]; and the organization that sells or distributes the test" (Harris, 1985, p. 21). In addition, the Tennessee Higher Education Commission in Nashville has compiled a list of subject-matter tests (for both baccalaureate and associate degree programs) that have been approved by faculty members and the state's governing and coordinating board staffs (Harris, 1985).

The Graduate Record Examination (GRE) is perhaps the most widely used standardized assessment of the knowledge students have acquired in their major. Seniors at both the University of Tennessee at Knoxville and Northeast Missouri State University take GRE field tests (where applicable) as part of the larger assessment program. The range of subject tests encompasses biology, chemistry, computer science, economics, education, engineering, French, geology, history, literature in English, mathematics, music, physics, political science, psychology, sociology, and Spanish (Harris, 1985). Harris (1985) has pointed out, however, that these tests originally were targeted at screening candidates for graduate and professional schools. As predictors of future performance, then, they stress individual differences, a feature which poses difficulties when the tests are used for program evaluation or assessment of the accomplishment of intended educational outcomes. Recently, the University of Tennessee at Knoxville has begun to pilot new 1-hour Field Area Tests for ETS in the same fields as the GRE. These shorter examinations—when normed—will alleviate the problems associated with traditional GRE norms. Furthermore, they will yield additional subscores and offer greater flexibility in administration.

ACT's Proficiency Examination Program (PEP) presents another alternative. Initially commissioned for the External Degree Program of the Board of Regents of the State University of New York, these examinations are offered through the American College Testing Program outside New York State. Varying in length from 3 to 7 hours, they assess proficiency for award of college credit in the following academic areas: arts and sciences (11 subjects); business (18 subjects); education (4 subjects); nursing, associate level (8 subjects); and nursing, baccalaureate level (8 subjects). (Harris, 1985). Once again, Harris accompanied his explanation with a caveat: "The PEP Examinations are designed to reflect the content of individual courses rather than programs. Therefore, they will be of limited value in overall assessment of major programs, and it would be both administratively awkward and expensive to use these examinations for program assessment" (p. 22).

The College-Level Examination Program (CLEP) mentioned previously also comprises some 33 subject examinations, several of which include optional free response or essay sections. However, the primary objective of these tests is to assess proficiency in lower-division college courses, not the "comprehensive proficiency expected of a graduating senior in a major field" (Harris, 1985, p. 22). Hence, Harris had advised against employing these 90-minute examinations solely for program evaluation purposes.

Yet another entree from the ETS menu is the Defense Activity for Non-Traditional Education Support (DANTES) achievement tests. In some ways similar to CLEP, DANTES examines only the equivalent of one semester's work and covers different subject areas, including science (9 subjects); social science (11 subjects); business (7 subjects); applied technology (14 subjects); languages (4 subjects); and mathematics (7 subjects). Although untimed, the tests can be completed in approximately 90 minutes (Harris, 1985).

Business programs may wish to consider the newly minted, nationally normed examination devised by the American Assembly of Collegiate Schools of Business (AACSB). Finally, a long-term ETS project involving the development of "item-banked" tests in such fields as agriculture, psychology, and criminology will eventually provide a common set of core questions in those subjects for all institutions along with a separate pool of items allowing local customization.

Local Alternatives

Locally constructed instruments aimed at program improvement through assessing the accomplishment of intended educational outcomes have arisen out of necessity—"in the absence of available standardized alternatives" (Ewell, 1987, p. 18). In one of the country's most widely acclaimed programs, the University of Tennessee at Knoxville (UTK) combines some 45 faculty-developed instruments with the GRE's standardized tests to measure the competencies of various departmental majors. A number of readily obtainable publications by UTK's Instructional Evaluation Program Coordinator, Trudy Banta, and her colleagues extensively discuss this nationally recognized assessment program together with the process of test evolution. Among Banta's most recent contributions are "Using Faculty-Developed Exit Examinations to Evaluate Academic Programs," in the January/February 1988 issue of the *Journal of Higher Education*, and "Performance Funding in Tennessee: Stimulus for Program Improvement," in Halpern's (1987) *Student Outcomes Assessment: What Institutions Stand to Gain*. In addition, a comprehensive bibliography of assessment materials is available through UTK's Assessment Resource Center, which welcomes serious inquiries into its work.

Other locally designed examinations have emerged from "dissatisfaction with the match in content and coverage between available standardized tests and the curriculum" (Ewell, 1987, p. 18). Among the prime examples are an experimental sophomore-junior project at King's College (Pennsylvania) and pilot activities at Berea, Carson-Newman, and Mars Hill colleges testing institutionally prepared written and oral examinations for senior English, religion/philosophy, and political science majors (Weiner, 1987). The Plattsburg campus of the State University of New York currently is developing tests in major disciplines for several schools in the SUNY system.

At Indiana University of Pennsylvania, an innovative program known as the Pre-Teacher Assessment Project employs trained teacher-evaluators to assess sophomore education majors on each of 13 skill dimensions: planning and organizing, monitoring, leadership, sensitivity, problem analysis, strategic decision making, tactical decision making, oral communication, oral presentation, written communication, innovativeness, tolerance for stress, and initiative. Among the vehicles for this evaluation are videotaped scenarios, teaching simulations, and organization of an educational fair (Orr, 1987).

Thus, the prevailing assessment mode has brought higher education full circle. As Ewell (1987) has pointed out, recent "pressures for enhanced assessment have stimulated colleges and universities to reexamine the senior comprehensive—in general education or, more commonly, in the major field—as an alternative to standardized testing" (p. 18). An integral component of the curriculum and, more significantly, the gateway to graduation, the traditional senior comprehensive examination "entailed objective demonstration of a student's mastery of core concepts and material . . . [and] application of these concepts to an extensive critical essay or problem-solving exercise" (Ewell, 1987, p. 18). However, in contrast to the institutional effectiveness paradigm advanced in this *Handbook*, the "primary intent . . . was to determine what students knew and not to identify the strengths and weaknesses of the curriculum" (Ewell, 1987, p. 18).

To Buy or Not to Buy?

Arguments favoring the use of standardized versus locally developed major subject tests echo those presented on pages 72 through 73. Nationally normed and less susceptible to charges of subjectivity, standardized examinations also may prove poor measures of a particular department's intended educational outcomes. Although local examinations can easily be customized, they, in turn, consume faculty time and yield no external norms. Ultimately, the best advice is to carefully compare intended educational outcomes for the department or program with the material examined on each standardized test prior to reaching this crucial decision. And, there is no single "correct" solution. Whether the choice is to buy or to build a test, the appropriate answer will vary from field to field within an institution.

Professional Licensing: Is There a Doctor in the House?

As just suggested, a number of professional licensing and certification examinations routinely taken by students are readily available assessment material. Prospective attorneys agonize until receiving official results of their state's bar examination; likewise, accounting majors anxiously approach the rigorous certified public accountants (CPA) examination. Physicians, nurses, and other health care professionals also are subject to national and state licensing board requirements, for instance, examination by the National League of Nursing. And, state and local mandates for teacher education reform have culminated in use of the ETS National Teachers Examination as a rite of professional passage into many classrooms. Departments and institutions keep close track of their graduates' performance on such measures, frequently vying with one another for the highest percentage of successful completions. Moreover, graduate schools of business, law, and medicine have access to students' entry scores on the

GMAT, LSAT, and MCAT, respectively. Still, licensure examinations raise the same bold warning flags as other standardized instruments: they may not faithfully follow the curriculum. Some CPA exams, for instance, comprise questions from practitioners as well as from academicians.

Toward Assessment of Learning with Proper Perspective

Gregory R. Anrig, president of the venerable Educational Testing Service, ironically has cautioned that although individual institutions may find ETS (and similar standardized) examinations "helpful," externally imposed tests actually may prove detrimental. He continues, " 'There is not a consensus about what the core of learning should be,' making it difficult to develop *a quality test* [emphasis added] to be used for institutions in an entire state" (Anrig quoted in Jaschik, 1985, p. 16). Thus, experts would bet that institutions will not be satisfied with only one of the many assessment measures outlined in this *Handbook*. Recall that Trenton State College applied the ACT COMP and TGE simultaneously; faculty and administrators at that institution could find no single test "that evaluate[d] all the skills and understandings they considered important" (Curry & Hager, 1987, p. 59). Alverno College, Northeast Missouri State University, and the University of Tennessee at Knoxville are just several of the other institutions currently combining multiple methods—and doing so successfully. Within a particular field, multiple cognitive measures such as standardized and local written examinations, oral examinations, portfolio analyses, and demonstrations yield a more thorough picture of effectiveness than any single instrument alone.

Whatever the method(s) of assessment, Marchese (1987) has reminded us that the process invariably entails judgment by external parties—faculty members reviewing achievement across courses, outside examiners, or even the producers of standardized instruments. "Somebody beyond the agent of instruction [often an accrediting team] is asking the questions, What does it add up to? What was learned? Is that good enough?" (p. 7). Institutions, however, must move beyond those queries, investing the answers toward enhancing instruction, educational outcomes, and, in turn, their effectiveness. "Assessment *per se* guarantees nothing by way of improvement, no more than a thermometer cures a fever" (Marchese, 1987, p. 8). Faculty and administrators who respond to the assessment siren with "a data-gathering effort only" have missed the whole point and set themselves up for the proverbial fall (Marchese, 1987). Yes, cognitive assessment *does* involve testing. But, evidence of an institution's true commitment to assessment does not emerge from an impressive slate of examinations alone; the real proof lies in its reply to the question Where do we go from here? In the oft-imitated song, Sam Cooke claims, "I don't know much about history . . . biology . . . a science book . . . or the French I took." Colleges and universities can easily verify such statements through testing. However, what they subsequently do with that information will determine their ultimate effectiveness. The first three letters in *cognitive* represent an important point about the assessment of learning: it is just one component of a much larger process; the other pieces of the paradigm ensure that the results will be analyzed and judiciously applied.

References: Cited and Recommended

Carroll, L. (1960). *Alice through the looking-glass*. New York: Bramhall House. (Original work published 1871).

Curry, W., & Hager, E. (1987). Assessing general education: Trenton State College. In D. F. Halpern (Ed.), *Student outcomes assessment: What institutions stand to gain* (pp. 57–65). New Directions in Higher Education, no. 59, XV(3). San Francisco: Jossey-Bass.

Ewell, P. T. (1987). Establishing a campus-based assessment program. In D. F. Halpern (Ed.), *Student outcomes assessment: What institutions stand to gain* (pp. 9–24). New Directions in Higher Education, no. 59, XV(3).

Halpern, D. F. (1987a). Recommendations and caveats. In D. F. Halpern (Ed.), *Student outcomes assessment: What institutions stand to gain* (pp. 109–111). New Directions in Higher Education, no. 59, XV(3).

Halpern, D. F. (1987b). Student outcomes assessment: Introduction and overview. In D. F. Halpern (Ed.), *Student outcomes assessment: What institutions stand to gain* (pp. 5–8). New Directions in Higher Education, no. 59, XV(3).

Harris, J. (1985). Assessing outcomes in higher education. In C. Adelman (Ed.), *Assessment in American higher education: Issues and contexts* (pp. 13–31). Washington, DC: U.S. Department of Education.

Hartle, T. W. (1985). The growing interest in measuring the educational achievement of college students. In C. Adelman (Ed.), *Assessment in American higher education: Issues and contexts* (pp. 1–11). Washington, DC: U.S. Department of Education.

Jaschik, S. (1985, September 18). Public universities trying tests and surveys to measure what students learn. *Chronicle of Higher Education*, pp. 1, 16.

Marchese, T. J. (1987). Third down, ten years to go. *AAHE Bulletin*, 40(4), 3–8.

Orr, J. (1987, September 29). Pre-teacher assessment: Plan to upgrade teaching quality. Indiana (PA) *Gazette*, p. 13.

Resnick, D. P., & Goulden, M. (1987). Assessment, curriculum, and expansion: A historical perspective. In D. F. Halpern (Ed.), *Student outcomes assessment: What institutions stand to gain* (pp. 77–88). New Directions in Higher Education, no. 59, *XV*(3).

Weiner, J. R. (1987). *National directory: Assessment programs and projects.* Washington, DC: AAHE Assessment Forum.

Assessment-Related Information from Institutional Data Systems

Bobby H. Sharp

Institutions of higher learning routinely maintain and report vast amounts of data about themselves. Thus, during the "Conduct of Inventory of Assessment Procedures" phase (see Figure 4, p. 26), one source of potentially useful information about an institution already exists in a form that does not require the development or adoption of tests or surveys. It is entirely possible that some of the best evidence of how well institutional goals included in the Expanded Statement of Institutional Purpose have been accomplished resides in institutions' own data systems. When existing institutional data are supplemented with additional data from tests and surveys, appropriate measures of institutional effectiveness can be produced.

Purpose of the Resource Section

The purposes of this resource section are

1. To review currently maintained institutional data that may be used as indicators of institutional effectiveness;
2. To critique limitations of typical institutions' data systems when called upon to support outcomes assessment;
3. To suggest ways for increasing the value of data systems to assessment activities.

Given the variety of institutional data systems, an objective of this resource section is to stimulate individuals involved in institutional effectiveness and outcomes assessment to evaluate the usefulness of their own institutions' data systems. When inadequacies are found in data systems, modifications to the systems may be feasible to assist such efforts more readily.

Basic Assumption

This resource section is predicated upon a basic assumption that is emphasized throughout this publication and depicted graphically in Figures 4 and 6:

> For existing institutional data to contribute meaningfully to outcomes assessment, those data must be fundamentally linked to appropriate statements of intention by the institution and its various units.

Within the context of institutional effectiveness, institutional data tell little in and of themselves. The meaningfulness of data derives directly from their link to specific statements of intention that have been composed within the whole system of institutional effectiveness and assessment activities. The mere ability to generate impressive amounts of data is of secondary importance to the appropriateness of the data in helping an institution tell if it is accomplishing its stated intentions at the departmental and institutional levels.

Typical Institutional Data and Reporting Systems

Most institutional data systems reflect the two primary types of activities or processes they were designed to support.

Operational Support

Routine institutional activities such as registering students, collecting and recording student fee payments, maintaining accurate student records, and meeting faculty and staff payrolls have been quite suited to automating with the use of computers. These data systems obviously provide valuable support to institutions in carrying out essential operations. However, the initial implementation of these data systems was largely to provide operational data to support transactions that routinely occur as part of institutional functioning.

For that reason, their usefulness to institutional effectiveness may be limited to those stated outcomes or objectives that pertain to operating procedures and practices. Examples of how transactional data systems can support institutional effectiveness include the assessment statements of intended objectives by

1. Financial units that are charged with effective budget control, accounting, and financial reporting practices of an institution;
2. A Registrar's Office charged with the mechanics of the registration process, prompt production of class rolls, and timely release of student grades;
3. An Office of Financial Aid responsible for the timeliness and fairness of financial aid awards.

Decision Support

A second area where traditional data systems provide useful data is in the support of process decisions. Examples include data used to support decisions in such areas as

1. Admissions and institutional marketing,
2. Student retention efforts,
3. Faculty hiring practices,
4. Faculty workload and productivity,
5. Faculty salaries,
6. Space utilization,
7. Course and program offerings,
8. Academic and support services (e.g., library holdings).

The importance of such data was confirmed by El-Khawas (1986), who reported that the vast majority of administrators responding to the American Council on Education survey on practices in higher education included many of those data as appropriate measures of institutional effectiveness.

As with data support of transactional activities, data used to support process decisions throughout an institution also may be valuable in assisting an institution in its institutional effectiveness and outcomes assessment activities. The usefulness of data such as the examples in the previous paragraph depends largely on how statements of institutional and departmental intentions relate to the institution's decision processes. Such data, for instance, may reveal a great deal about the extent to which an institution accomplishes its intentions regarding effective resource use and allocation.

Federal Reports

Where institutional or departmental intentions pertain to typical operational and decision processes, the data to support the assessment of those objectives are readily available at most institutions. For many years institutions of higher learning regularly have provided numerous reports to the federal government. Once part of the Higher Education General Information Surveys (HEGIS) system of reports, one set of reports is now collected by the Center for Educational Statistics as the Integrated Postsecondary Education Data System (IPEDS). The purpose of HEGIS/IPEDS has been to obtain general information about institutions—who attends and who graduates, what programs are offered and what programs are completed, and the human and financial resources used in providing higher education services. In addition to HEGIS/IPEDS reports, other reports have been routinely submitted to various federal agencies such as the Office of Civil Rights (OCR), the Office of Vocational and Adult Education (OVAE), the Office of Postsecondary Education (OPE), and the Equal Employment Opportunity Commission (EEOC).

Because on many campuses several offices have shared responsibilities for submitting the HEGIS/IPEDS and other federal reports, one of the first tasks may be to assemble copies of these reports into a complete set for use in the assessment process. These reports contain a considerable amount of information concerning students, faculty, and finances, and taken together, represent a rich historical data source for use in an institutional effectiveness program. In addition, these reports represent a concerted effort to adhere, over time, to consistent and standard data definitions, adding reliability to the information contained in them.

State and System Reports

To supplement the reports submitted to federal agencies, state and system agencies often require their own data reports. These reports should also be assembled and reviewed for their usefulness to the assessment program. These reports, like those submitted to HEGIS/IPEDS, typically have been developed through thought and deliberation, lending credibility to their contents.

Internal Reports

Another source for decision support information that may be useful to a program of institutional assessment includes the myriad of both routine and ad hoc studies and reports produced within every institution. These studies range widely and include such subjects as admissions practices (e.g., rates of applications, acceptances, and matriculation), graduation rates, affirmative action practices (e.g., hiring, promoting, and terminating practices), faculty flows, and faculty salaries. As expected of internal studies, the level of sophistication and the usefulness of these reports vary substantially from institution to institution. Part of the "inventory of assessment procedures" phase (see Figure 4) nevertheless should involve compiling—and in some instances, reconciling, where incongruous figures exist because of the application of different definitions or procedures—an inventory of the internal studies available.

Limitations of Traditional Data Systems

Cross-Sectional Orientation

Despite the vast amount of data maintained and reported by institutions, many data systems have an inherent weakness when called upon to support assessment. That weakness is the cross-sectional orientation of typical data elements and report formats associated with those data systems.

Institutional "census files," from which many of the reports mentioned thus far are generated, typically represent snapshots of operational files. As such, they show what the operational files contained at an instant in time. Historical snapshots are not updated as institutional data change. The operational files, however, constantly change as fields of data are overwritten with "new" data. Because operational files usually were designed to support routine institutional operations, the data elements and the snapshots produced from those elements are limited to cross-sectional and time series measures of institutional processes. Such measures, of course, can be of considerable value to institutions as evidence of progress toward goals.

Longitudinal Orientation

Institutional effectiveness and outcomes assessment, however, primarily require at least some additional information that follows institutional processes and products (i.e., students) over time. For data systems to support fully efforts to assess outcomes and to measure institutional effectiveness, they must include longitudinal orientations. This will particularly apply to student data. Progress of individuals through their educational programs can best be shown when various measures of their performance are collected and maintained across successive time periods. Built-in referents for measuring progress then exist. Traditional data systems thus may require modification or supplementation in order to provide adequately the longitudinal orientation crucial to outcomes assessment.

Student Data Elements Supportive of Outcomes Assessment

The particular data elements used to support outcomes assessment necessarily will depend upon an institution's assessment program. However, for most institutions, there are at a minimum two types of student data elements that can be maintained and will be expected:

1. *Demographic data elements*—These typically will come from admissions and student attribute data files and may not change throughout the tracking period. Included here are such variables as the following:
   a. Student identifier
   b. Birth date
   c. Race
   d. Sex
   e. Entrance test scores
   f. High school grades
   g. High school rank
   h. Prior institution(s) attended
   i. Prior degree(s) earned
   j. Proposed major and degree
   k. Predicted college success measures (e.g., predicted grade point average)

These data elements both broaden the scope of outcomes analysis and offer referents against which progress may be measured.

2. *Academic process data elements*—"Term" files usually provide most of these data elements. That is, these data elements are term specific, varying from one term to the next. Examples of these data elements include the following:
   a. Declared major(s) and minor(s)
   b. Financial aid and tuition status
   c. Current course-taking data (e.g., number, name, section, credit hours, grade)
   d. Grade point average or quality points
   e. Graduation data, when available

These data elements allow the tracking of academic performance by term. Among questions answered by such a collection of data elements are those related to the history of majors declared as well as the calculation of retention/attrition and graduation rates. Data are then available to assess the progress of an entire cohort, a subgroup, or even an individual student.

Most institutional data systems are fairly well equipped to provide the demographic and academic process data elements just identified. The primary task would be to extract them and assemble them into a longitudinally designed file.

Such a file, however, still lacks additional academic process data elements critical to the success of an assessment program. Increasingly, institutions are collecting a considerable amount of data from attitudinal surveys and cognitive tests. Other sections of this chapter address the development and use of these instruments within outcomes assessment. In reality, the results of these surveys and tests also measure academic progress and should be incorporated and used along with those process-type data elements previously listed.

Using Institutional Data Systems in Assessment

How institutional data systems are used in assessment of institutional effectiveness depends upon several factors.

1. The extent to which data systems are automated will either limit or expand the opportunities for their use. During systematic outcomes assessment over time, a considerable amount of data will be collected for analysis. Sufficient and accessible automated storage will be essential. Powerful, easily used data analysis tools (e.g., statistical packages) will be necessities. Limited computing facilities simply may be overburdened by extensive longitudinal data files, thereby constraining users of longitudinal data. As has been demonstrated by Ewell (1987) and others, however, modest but quite effective longitudinal tracking files can be built using microcomputers with sufficient magnetic storage.
2. As implied in Chapter 1, the way assessment data will be used depends upon the commitment of institutional leaders to the entire institutional effectiveness and outcomes assessment program. The best possible assessment data will be of little use to an institution when the initial question why has not been addressed. To

get the most use out of assessment data, institutions must have thoughtfully articulated why they are collecting it in the first place.
3. Potential users of assessment data must be taught how those data can be used. Thinking in terms of longitudinal data collection and analysis is a relatively novel approach. As a new way of measuring the effectiveness of all aspects of institutions, institutional effectiveness or outcomes assessment data require the development of users' understanding of how longitudinal data may be utilized. However, once involved in applying sound assessment practices, users will see benefits of this approach and explore new uses for the collected data.

Possible uses of institutional data systems in assessment are numerous. Many have been suggested and alluded to already in this resource section. Thus, those offered in the following section are but a few among many.

Calculating Retention and Graduation Rates

In El-Khawas's (1986) report, 88% of those higher education administrators surveyed indicated that retention and graduation rates were appropriate measures of institutional effectiveness. Their appropriateness, as emphasized throughout this publication, depends upon the statements of institutional and departmental intentions that have been formulated. For most institutions, however, facilitating the successful progress of students through academic programs to graduation represents a fundamental purpose for their existence. Measuring the extent to which students persist to graduation thus may offer indications of how effectively institutions have accomplished one of their fundamental purposes.

Thorough analysis of retention and graduation rates can best be conducted by using a longitudinal-oriented data system. Then cohorts of students entering the enrollment "pipeline" can be followed as long as information on them is deemed important to the assessment program.

Questions about retention and graduation rates usually require disaggregation into subgroups. That is, it is one thing to know that a certain percentage of entering full-time freshmen will persist to graduation, but it is quite another to know retention and graduation rates of student subgroups. These disaggregated retention and graduation rates provide institutions with considerably more useful information in answering pertinent questions, such as

1. For an entering freshmen cohort, how do retention and graduation rates differ among ethnic groups?
2. How do retention and graduation rates differ among majors?
3. How do retention and graduation rates differ among ethnic groups within majors?
4. If there are differences that cause concern, how can anyone know if strategies adopted to deal with the issue are working?

The ability to answer questions such as these may determine the success or failure of institutional effectiveness and assessment programs.

The questions posed in the preceding paragraph reemphasize the importance of having a carefully designed longitudinal data system. Systems that permit answering only the first or second question (i.e., regarding rates for ethnic groups or for majors), but not the third (i.e., rates for ethnic groups within majors), may be limited in their usefulness. The extent of the disaggregation should be considered in conjunction with the levels of cross analysis anticipated.

Comparing Successive Test Scores and Inventory Results

Some institutions have begun employing batteries of cognitive tests as part of their assessment plan. Institutions promoting a "value-added" concept of higher education, for example, must develop means to demonstrate it. One way to demonstrate value-added has been to require standardized test scores for students at different points in their educational experience. Thus, entering freshmen, rising juniors, and graduating seniors may be required to take standardized tests and have their scores maintained in longitudinal data systems.

Taken individually, the test scores offer little evidence of value-added education. Compared over time, however, the results of the exams may indeed serve as measures of educational progress and may stimulate changes in such areas as curricula and course offerings.

Along with cognitive tests, opinion and attitudinal surveys may be administered over successive time periods and may serve as useful indicators of educational progress. Differences in responses between the point of entry as freshmen and the point of exit as graduates can tell institutions how students perceive their own progress vis-à-vis the academic and support programs offered to them. The capacity to compare successive inventory results, though, presupposes some kind of longitudinal data system.

In comparing both cognitive test scores and inventory results over time, institutions should remember that the focus is on *institutional effectiveness*, not individual student performance. The purpose of various tests and inventories administered to students is to assess the effectiveness of institutions and their subunits. As a part of an assessment system, the results of the tests and inventories should be used by institutions to set policies for more effectively reaching their intended outcomes and objectives.

Determining Course-Taking Patterns

A longitudinal data system that retains students' course enrollment histories also can provide quite useful information about educational progress. When considered along with other assessment indicators such as retention and graduation rates or cognitive test scores, the results obtained can be especially useful in several ways. For instance, information learned from relating graduating students' cognitive test scores to their course-taking patterns may help improve

1. Curricular requirements/offerings,
2. Student advising programs,
3. Course offerings,
4. Faculty teaching assignments,
5. Space allocation.

Results of such an analysis thus range from happier, more successful students to improved use of institutional resources.

Providing Interinstitutional Follow-up Information on Students

Among the data elements within longitudinal data systems that support assessment are those pertaining to activities of students following graduation. Over 80% of the administrators responding to El-Khawas's (1986) survey indicated that "honors and other achievements of recent graduates," "job placement rates of graduates, by field," and "graduates' performance on the job" each were appropriate measures of institutional effectiveness.

Equally important indicators of institutional effectiveness, however, are the graduates who successfully continue their education at other institutions; for example:

1. Two-year institutions whose missions include preparing students to complete their baccalaureate degrees at four-year institutions

need to know how their graduates perform at the senior institutions.

2. Four-year institutions need to know how their baccalaureate graduates perform when they enroll in graduate programs.
3. Graduate-level institutions with master's degree programs need to know how their graduates perform in doctoral degree programs.

To support assessment, then, institutions at all levels should prepare for providing "feeder" institutions and programs with follow-up information on their former students. Longitudinal data systems containing data elements for prior institutions attended and prior degrees obtained, along with current status and performance measures, will facilitate the interinstitutional cooperation required. Regular reports provided to feeder institutions can then become part of the longitudinal data systems supportive of those institutions' assessment programs.

The provision of such data to feeder institutions is authorized under USCS 1232g, Family Educational and Privacy Act:

(F) Organizations conducting studies for, or on behalf of, educational agencies or institutions for the purpose of developing, validating, or administering predictive tests, administering student aid programs, and improving instruction, if such studies are conducted in such a manner as will not permit the personal identification of students and their parents by persons other than representatives of such organizations and such information will be destroyed when no longer needed for the purpose for which it is conducted;

(G) Accrediting organizations in order to carry out their accrediting functions.

This release of the student data to feeder institutions is premised upon their use for "improving instruction" as part of institutional effectiveness. The limitations regarding use of the data and protection of the individual student's identification to unauthorized persons must be strictly enforced.

Summary

Successful efforts to assess institutional effectiveness must be supported by appropriate data systems. For most institutions, a considerable amount of useful data already exists and only (!) requires cataloging and drawing into suitable formats. Examples of these data are the many federal, state, system, and internal reports regularly produced over many years. These existing reports may be quite helpful in demonstrating institutional progress toward stated goals.

Many institutions, however, will find that their data systems lack a sufficiently longitudinal orientation to fully support their assessment of institutional effectiveness. Inherent in measuring institutional effectiveness is the capability for following the progress of students over time. Data systems must be configured to support longitudinal analyses relating demographics to academic performance and personal development. Research such as calculating retention and graduation rates, comparing cognitive test scores over time, analyzing course-taking patterns, and providing interinstitutional follow-up data on students will then be facilitated. Although the commitment of resources to adapt, supplement, or otherwise expand institutional data systems to support institutional effectiveness may not have been initially considered in implementation of institutional effectiveness, depending on the institution's and departments' statements of intentions, expenditures to utilize existing data more fully to meet assessment needs may be among the most cost-effective actions that an institution can take.

References: Cited and Recommended

Criteria for accreditation: Commission on colleges. (1984). Atlanta, GA: Southern Association of Colleges and Schools.

El-Khawas, E. (1986). *Campus trends, 1986* (Higher Education Panel Report No. 73). Washington, DC: American Council on Education.

Ewell, P. T. (1987a). Establishing a campus-based assessment program. In D. F. Halpern (Ed.), *Student outcomes assessment: What institutions stand to gain* (pp. 9–24). New Directions in Higher Education, no. 59, XV(3). San Francisco: Jossey-Bass.

Ewell, P. T. (1987b). Principles of longitudinal enrollment analysis: Conducting retention and student flow studies. In J. Muffo & G. W. McLaughlin (Eds.), *A primer on institutional research* (pp. 1–19). Tallahassee, FL: Association for Institutional Research.

Harris, J. (1985). *Assessing outcomes in higher education: Practical suggestions for getting started. Unpublished manuscript, David Lipscomb College, Nashville, TN.*

Howard, R. D., Nichols, J. O., & Gracie, L. W. (1987). Institutional research support of the self-study. In J. Muffo & G. W. McLaughlin (Eds.), *A primer on institutional research* (pp. 79–88). Tallahassee, FL: Association for Institutional Research.

Kauffman, J. F. (1984). Assessing the quality of student services. In R. A. Scott (Ed.), *Determining the effectiveness of campus services* (pp. 23–36). New

Directions in Institutional Research, no. 41, *XI*(1). San Francisco: Jossey-Bass.

Keller, G. (1983). *Academic strategy* (see especially pp. 131–133). Baltimore: Johns Hopkins University Press.

Klepper, W. M., Nelson, J. E., & Miller, T. E. (1987). In M. M. Stodt & W. M. Klepper (Eds.), *Increasing retention: Academic and student affairs administrators in partnership* (pp. 27–37). New Directions in Higher Education, no. 60, *XV*(4). San Francisco: Jossey-Bass.

Miller, R. I. (1981). Appraising institutional performance. In P. Jedamus, M. W. Peterson, & Associates (Eds.), *Improving academic management* (pp. 406–431). San Francisco: Jossey-Bass.

Mingle, J. R. (1985). *Measuring the educational achievement of undergraduates: State and national developments.* Unpublished manuscript, State Higher Education Executive Officers, Denver.

Terenzini, P. T. (1987). Studying student attrition and retention. In J. Muffo & G. W. McLaughlin (Eds.), *A primer on institutional research* (pp. 20–35). Tallahassee, FL: Association for Institutional Research.

CHAPTER FOUR

Detailed Design at the Departmental Level

The activities accomplished at the institutional level during the first year of the process are preparatory to the majority of the campus's efforts toward implementation of institutional effectiveness or outcomes assessment that will take place within the academic and administrative departments beginning in the second year of implementation (see Figure 7). As in so many other instances, ultimate success in institutional effectiveness implementation is dependent upon the service provided to the institution's constituents (students, alumni, etc.) by its operating elements (departments/programs).

Among the more difficult tasks that must be accomplished in implementation during this second year is gaining the confidence and active support of academic and administrative department chairpersons and/or heads. What are the obstacles to be overcome in gaining this confidence and support?

Probably the first obstacle is the "inertia" of academic and administrative practices, which have for years focused almost exclusively upon the processes that take place in a department rather than the end "results" or outcomes to which those departmental processes contribute. In the academic sector, these processes relate to class scheduling, grade reporting, and so forth. Within administrative departments, process-oriented activities such as conducting registration, acquiring books, cutting the grass, and preparing the payroll all seem more familiar and urgent than outcomes assessment.

Second, implementation of institutional effectiveness will be an additional task rather than a replacement for any of the process-oriented tasks required in continuation of day-to-day operations. This will be a particularly difficult obstacle to overcome at relatively

Figure 7

**The Second Year of a Four-Year Plan for
Implementation of Institutional Effectiveness
and Assessment Activities on a Campus**

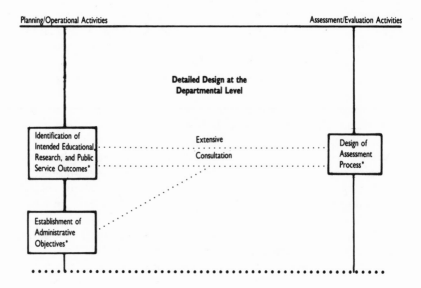

*Resource Section included in chapter to support

smaller institutions or in smaller departments within larger institutions, where the departmental-level administrative personnel may already be overburdened with process-oriented requirements for which little release time or support is provided.

A third major obstacle to departmental leadership support will, in all likelihood, be a large measure of skepticism regarding implementation of institutional effectiveness as just another fad or redirection of effort and doubt about the institution's commitment to following through with implementation. Many departmental administrators have witnessed the great fanfare surrounding announcements of significant institutional initiatives in the past, which proved to be only lip service.

Given these obstacles, winning the confidence and active support of departmental administrators for implementation will take a concerted effort. However, this confidence can be stimulated by the following:

1. Visible commitment in word and deed by the institution's CEO and Chief Academic Officer (CAO)
2. Complete and professionally executed staff work at the institutional level during the first year of implementation
3. Implementation plans that identify each department as one component of an ongoing project involving other departments and extending into the future
4. Presence of an external stimulus, such as an accrediting agency, requiring implementation

Gaining the active support of departmental administrators will require their choice of institutional effectiveness implementation over, or at least along with, their process-oriented responsibilities. Such a choice will doubtlessly require the extension of various incentives for implementation, such as those referenced earlier in Chapter 2. However, it is also important that the institution avoid apparent punishment of those units in which implementation is not being aggressively pursued.

Although activities on the planning/operational and assessment/ evaluation tracks remained relatively separate during the first year of implementation, extensive coordination between such activities is required in the second year. As the various academic and administrative departments go about establishment of their intended outcomes and administrative objectives, it is important that the departments identify (in general) the means through which assessment of their actual results will take place. At the same time, those parties designing the institution's assessment/evaluation process need to be well informed regarding the objectives on which that process will focus. Neither the interests of the planning/operational track nor those of the assessment/evaluation track should be paramount in this relationship. Rather, a give-and-take process should occur between the two, yielding the most appropriate intended departmental/program outcomes or objectives that can be supported by a feasible assessment plan.

Planning/Operational Activities

During this second year of implementation, planning/operational activities are extended to the departmental/program level through establishment of "Intended Educational (Instructional), Research, and Service Outcomes/Objectives" in academic and administrative departments.

All of these results-oriented statements should be carefully linked to support of the institution's expanded statement of purpose (see Figure 8). On some campuses, the Expanded Statement of Institutional Purpose will be utilized as the starting point, and results-oriented statements will flow "down" from this statement to the individual departments. At other institutions, departmental/program statements of intentions will be directed "up" to support the Expanded Statement of Institutional Purpose. Whether these results-oriented statements are voluntarily originated by the institution's departments or are directed from a central level, it is imperative that a clear and identifiable linkage be established between the expanded statement of purpose and such departmental results-oriented statements of intentions.

In the instructional area, results-oriented statements of intentions will primarily take the form of "Intended Educational Outcomes" by degree program offered. It may also be desirable to establish separate statements of intended outcomes regarding educational programs (such as general education, premedicine, or certificate programs) not resulting in a specific degree.

Additionally, intended outcomes should be identified for the other two traditional areas included in statements of purpose (research and public service). These statements of "Intended Research and Public Service Outcomes" should be linked to the Expanded Statement of Institutional Purpose.

Figure 8

Undergraduate English Program

Example of Linkage between
Expanded Statement of Institutional Purpose,
Departmental/Program Intended Outcomes/Objectives, and
Assessment Criteria and Procedures at Our University

**Expanded Statement of
Institutional Purpose**

Mission Statement: The principal focus of Our University's curricular program is undergraduate education in the liberal arts and sciences combined with a number of directly career related and preprofessional fields.

Goal Statements: Each graduate of Our University will be treated as an individual, and all graduates of baccalaureate-level programs at the University will have developed a depth of understanding in their major field and been afforded the opportunity to prepare for a career or profession following graduation.

**Departmental/Program
Intended Outcomes/Objectives**

1. Students completing the baccalaureate program in English will compare very favorably in their knowledge of literature with those students applying for graduate work in the field nationally.

2. Graduates will be able to critique a brief draft essay, pointing out the grammatical, spelling, and punctuation errors and offering appropriate suggestions for correction of the deficiencies.

3. Students completing the baccalaureate program will be capable of writing a brief journal article and submitting it for publication.

**Assessment Criteria
& Procedures**

a. The average score of the graduates of the baccalaureate program in English on the "Literature in English" GRE subject test (which they will be required to take shortly before graduation) will be at or near the 50th percentile compared to national results.

b. Ninety percent of the graduates of the English baccalaureate program will "agree" or "strongly agree" with the statement "In the field of literature I feel as well prepared as the majority of individuals nationwide who have applied to graduate programs in English during the past year."

a. As part of a departmental comprehensive examination administered during the students' final semester prior to graduation, they will critique a short draft essay, identify grammatical, spelling, and punctuation errors; and offer suggestions for correction of the deficiencies. Eighty percent of the program's graduates will identify and offer suggestions for remediation of 90% of the errors in the draft essay.

a. All graduates of the baccalaureate-level program in English will prepare a journal article for submission and forward it to the English department.

b. Eighty percent of those journal articles submitted will be judged acceptable for publication by a jury of English department faculty.

c. Twenty percent of those articles submitted will be published in student or other publications.

Finally, the institution's administrative and educational support units should play a major role in accomplishment of institutional effectiveness through establishment of "Administrative Objectives" supporting the Expanded Statement of Institutional Purpose. Direct linkage with portions of the expanded institutional statement of purpose by some units (payroll, auditing, physical plant, etc.) may be difficult to achieve. In this case, the objectives established by these units should focus upon creation of an academic and administrative environment conducive to more direct support of the Expanded Statement of Institutional Purpose by other departments/programs. Nonetheless, such statements of objectives or intentions should be established in all institutional units.

In the resource section entitled "Setting Intended Educational (Instructional), Research, and Service Outcomes and Administrative Objectives" these concepts are discussed further (see pages 102–119). Appendix B contains a series of examples of results-oriented statements linked both to the sample Expanded Statement of Institutional Purpose contained in Appendix A and to the assessment procedures found in the second resource section in this chapter, which is entitled "Designing the Assessment Process" (see pages 120–138).

Assessment/Evaluation Activities

Based upon the institutional-level activity in the previous year (initial design and implementation of attitudinal surveys, inventory of existing assessment procedures, adjustments of institutional data systems, identification of cognitive tests, etc.), assessment/evaluation activities in this second year of implementation also shift to the departmental/program level.

By the beginning of the second year of implementation, those charged with implementing assessment procedures on the campus should be prepared to work closely with each department/program in identifying appropriate ways to assess accomplishment of the statements of intention being developed within the unit. These means of assessment will include the following:

1. Attitudinal measures
2. Measures of cognitive learning
3. Performance measures
4. Information drawn from the institution's automated files
5. Other means

Data from these sources will be derived from both locally developed and standardized instruments, tests, and procedures.

In the educational (instructional) sector of the institution, a wide variety of assessment means probably will be brought to bear on departmental/program statements of "Intended Educational Outcomes," although it should be understood that not all accomplishments identified in such statements can be measured or ascertained. Attitudinal surveys and more direct measures (counts of patrons, external funding received, library circulation, etc.) will predominate in the institution's administrative departments.

The resource section entitled "Designing the Assessment Process" contains not only a much more detailed review of the concepts just described but also a discussion of the importance of multiple assessment procedures for each intended outcome or objective, the design of feedback mechanisms, and logistical support of the assessment process.

Together with the second-year implementation activities illustrated in Figure 7, these two resource sections can be used to guide the final preparations for implementing institutional effectiveness operations the following year.

Setting Intended Educational; (Instructional), Research, and Service Outcomes and Administrative Objectives

Linda Pratt, Donald Reichard, Brenda Rogers

In identifying and defining intended outcomes/objectives and the assessment procedures for measuring those outcomes in instruction, research, public service, or the various administrative units, key factors to consider are the time and effort needed to develop the outcomes/objectives and to implement the assessment process. If the number of outcomes/objectives is too large or the assessment procedure is too cumbersome, the process is likely to be abandoned in midstream. As Miller (1980) indicated, "The process of collecting data should be established in such a way that it can continue beyond the first self-assessment as a routine function of the master planning and decision-making process" (p. 425). For this to occur, the outcomes/objectives and the related assessment procedures must be simple and must be directly related to the most important goals of the institution and of the individual unit. The number of such departmental statements of intentions should be reduced to those that can be addressed effectively in any single time period.

It is not necessary or even desirable for any unit of the institution to develop a comprehensive set of outcomes/objectives that describe every detail of the operations of that unit. Rather, each unit must identify the most important or key outcomes or objectives and concentrate on assessment of those outcomes. In practice, this may mean choosing outcomes/objectives related to an area identified as being troublesome, addressing only those related to new or revised initiatives, or selecting only those outcomes deemed absolutely essential to unit operations. As an example, a department with a faculty that has an excellent reputation in the teaching area might want to increase its emphasis on faculty research and publication. The department could identify the accomplishment and publication of significant research findings as an intended outcome but would not, at the same time, identify improvement in teaching as an area for increased emphasis. An alumni office that has had an excellent system for identifying and tracking graduates of the institution since 1960 might set as an objective the improvement of the database concerning pre-1960 alumni. Critical to the success of the effort is the identification of outcomes/ objectives judged important to the operation of the unit and linked as directly as possible to the Expanded Statement of Institutional Purpose.

Once a set of generalized departmental/program outcomes/ objectives has been identified, the next step is to refine and complete these statements for use in assessing institutional effectiveness. The format for describing intended outcomes/objectives varies according to the reference, but the questions to be answered remain constant:

1. Is the outcome/objective consistent with the institution's Expanded Statement of Institutional Purpose?
2. Is the outcome/objective written at a reasonable level of expectation?
3. Is the outcome/objective clear and measurable?
4. Is the outcome/objective written at a reasonable level of specificity?
5. Does the outcome/objective specify the time frame in which it will be accomplished?

Within the context of these general questions, there are many formats for presenting objectives. The National Laboratory for Higher Education (1974) recommended that an objective (or intended outcome) take the form of a single statement with the following elements:

1. Responsibility—what person or unit is responsible for carrying out the objective
2. Outcome (or result)—what is expected to occur
3. Time—when the goal will be completed
4. Measurement (or assessment)—what will be used to measure accomplishment of the objective

5. Performance standards—what level of attainment is required
6. Conditions—what conditions must be met before the objective can be accomplished

An example of an objective written in this format is the following:

> By fall of the 1992–93 academic year [*time*], the admissions office [*responsibility*]—assuming that there are tuition increases of no more than 7% [*condition*]—will enroll an entering class [*outcome or result*] of 1,200 [*performance standard*]; the number of full-time registrations will be used to verify achievement [*measurement*].

Translated into the format suggested by one regional accrediting association, the Commission on Colleges of the Southern Association of Colleges and Schools (SACS, 1987), this objective would need the following:

> Statement of Purpose—Our University will recruit students of high academic credentials.

> Expected Results (outcome/objective)—By fall of the 1992–93 academic year, Our University will select an entering class of 1,200 students from a pool of 3,200 applicants.

> Assessment Procedures—The number of full-time registrations for first-time freshmen in the fall and spring semesters combined, as indicated by the records in the Registrar's Office, and the number of applicants for admissions during those periods, as indicated by the records in the Office of Admissions, will constitute the basic data for assessment of the extent of accomplishment.

> Administration of Assessment Procedures—The Office of Institutional Research will report the number of entering freshmen and of applicants as a part of the regular fall enrollment report, and the Office of Admissions will compare these data.

> Use of Assessment Findings—The Office of Admissions will review the results on a yearly basis and, if the results are below expectation, either initiate procedures to increase the number and the quality of applicants, or raise the matter for consideration at the institutional level.

These are only two examples of formats for writing objectives. Each institution must identify a format that is compatible with its own-planning and evaluation system. The format itself is not as important as the elements included, and many perfectly acceptable statements of departmental/program intentions will not explicitly contain all of the elements suggested. The sample outcome/objective just described could have been presented in the form of a table or with separate paragraphs for each element, and the second could have been written as a single statement with all of the elements included.

One of the most challenging aspects of writing objectives and of identifying outcomes for higher education, particularly for administrative units, is the problem of selecting the assessment procedures to determine whether the intentions identified have been achieved. While in the process of developing new outcomes/objectives, the department or administrative unit can easily identify assessment procedures that will be so time- and resource-consuming that they will become an end in themselves and not a means of determining whether a specific outcome/objective has been achieved. If this occurs, the long-term result is likely to be abandonment of the process. Pratt and Reichard (1983) recommended developing, wherever possible, assessment procedures using existing institutional records such as registration records, logs of student or public contact, monthly or weekly records of books checked out of the library or any other records, particularly those that can be reduced to regular monthly, quarterly, or yearly reports. If such records are not available or if the existing records are not appropriate for assessing a particular outcome/objective, special reports must be developed. Even in this case, the more completely the assessment procedures can be incorporated into existing operations of a unit, the more likely the assessment is to be continued over the long term. In a few instances, the particular academic or administrative unit may wish to collect data through a special procedure such as a survey of students, faculty, alumni, or local business operators. If this form of assessment is undertaken, it should generally be regarded as a long-term, repetitive effort, with the initial survey data used to form a baseline for future studies as well as to answer immediate assessment needs. Institutions should seriously consider centralization of the logistical aspects of such surveys to avoid duplication of effort and excessive cost.

As the individual assessment plans are developed for each outcome/ objective, the use of subjective measures should not be entirely neglected. Although objective measures are generally easier to collect and less open to question, such measures are not appropriate in every case. As Miller (1980, pp. 425–426) indicated:

> . . .institutional evaluation should use objective data where available and purposeful but make no apologies for using subjective data. Or, it is better to be generally right than precisely wrong. Objective data is important, yet considerable variation exists in the availability and quality of such evidence. . . . The lack of "hard" data should not deter careful and systematic decision making about important institutional matters. Solid bases for decision making can be developed by using whatever hard data are available along with experience, judgment, and common sense. Important institutional process-type decisions often are made on much less.

Whatever the source of data and whatever the type of evidence available, the careful selection of educational, research, and service outcomes and administrative objectives is among the most important part of the process of assessment. If outcomes and objectives are important and meaningful to the department/program, if the assessment procedures are easily incorporated into ongoing operations, and if those procedures provide useful information that can be used to improve those operations, then the process is likely to be sustained over time.

Linkage to Statement of Purpose

The first step in implementing institutional effectiveness is the development of an institutional mission statement or statement of purpose, as described in the resource section by Yost in the preceding chapter. Clear statements of mission, as noted by Moore (1986), provide the yardstick against which effectiveness is measured. If mission statements are unclear, can supporting goal statements be much better? Perhaps so, perhaps not. Regardless of the degree of acceptance or clarity of mission statements, planning and evaluation activities at the unit level may need to proceed. The task of fitting institutional and departmental/program processes together may be most challenging under the best of circumstances.

In order to ensure linkage of institutional and department/program statements of intention, SACS suggests the development of a series of matrices that relate planning and evaluation components to each of the traditional areas of institutional mission (e.g., teaching, research, public service) as well as to an institution's major operational areas such as admissions, curriculum, instruction, faculty, library, physical resources, and so forth. Essential planning and evaluation components identified by SACS include the following:

1. The statement of institutional purpose
2. The definition of expected results (outcomes or objectives)
3. The description of appropriate means of evaluation
4. The assignment of responsibility for implementation
5. The description of the use of evaluation results (SACS, 1987, pp. 11–13)

There are, however, inherent difficulties in attempting to link mission statements, goal statements, and their related outcomes/objectives. In this regard, Fincher (1978, p. 4) noted, "Goals may not be present at the beginning of an activity or function, but they are believed to be a future state, destination, or end product that will help guide and direct the progression of that activity or function." Not all outcomes are intended, encouraged, planned, or anticipated. In fact, side effects may be as important as intended outcomes. Institutional effectiveness may on occasion be as concerned with movement in "the right direction" as with the measurable achievement of narrowly defined outcomes/objectives. Thus, although institutions must attempt to state clearly their missions, goals, and outcomes/objectives, they must also maintain sufficient flexibility to permit revisions as the process unfolds.

Linkage of mission and goal statements from the "top down" is probably preferable to linkage from the "bottom up" on many campuses. Certainly this type of linkage more nearly matches many familiar planning models. Such top-down linkage is more appropriate for institutions with clearly articulated mission statements, for smaller institutions, and for selected colleges or universities where the existence of a unique ethos is all-pervasive. Charismatic presidential leadership or strong traditions of centralized leadership may also increase the likelihood of common acceptance of a well-defined mission statement that guides the development of institutional goals as well as departmental/program statements of intentions.

On the other hand, the bottom-up linkage of goals to a statement of purpose may be more effective for some institutions. In larger research institutions with diverse missions and goals, the tradition of decentralized funding patterns and governance structures may mean that institutional missions emerge from the broad statements of intentions of a loose confederation of largely autonomous schools and departments. In these instances, mission statements spring from the activities of the institution's subunits. In many institutions a combination of bottom-up and top-down development may occur. For example, in large universities each school or college may develop goals for top-down use by departments while, at the same time, the amalgamation of the goals of the schools or colleges may drive the institution's statement of purpose in an essentially bottom-up process.

Setting Intended Educational (Instructional) Outcomes

At the level of the academic department, success in both establishing educational outcomes and attaining them is dependent on the faculty, who are the direct link to students and the educational process. Educational outcomes, defined as changes that result from instruction, must be focused on student learning and the improvement of teaching and learning. Specifically, academic departments must state in behavioral terms their expectations for student achievement. Because faculty have responsibility for developing the curriculum and courses, as well as for teaching and testing students, they should also be responsible for defining such reasonable expectations of students.

That faculty must be involved in setting educational outcomes for the academic departments is a fact accepted by virtually all members of the higher education community. For any other group to do so would be usurping this important role of the faculty. In fact, the threat to the faculty's academic freedom to select course content and instructional methods, to develop testing procedures, and to set grading standards is a major source of faculty resistance to the assessment movement in higher education.

The success of assessment efforts depends on more than focusing those efforts on academic departments, the curricula, and courses; it also depends on using the assessment results for improving the teaching and learning process. Faculty will be skeptical if they are not sure how the assessment information will be used. Who will have access to the departmental information, and how will they use it? Will programs be eliminated based on student outcomes? Will results be used to promote and terminate faculty? To minimize such legitimate concerns about the misuse of the assessment results, faculty must be involved at the planning stage during which the ground rules for use of the information are established. Unless faculty are assured that they will maintain some degree of control over use of the information at the academic department level, they may not provide the essential support in setting meaningful educational outcomes for their programs.

Thus, from the very beginning of the implementation process, the administration must include faculty in the decisions about assessment of institutional effectiveness. Faculty, representing a wide range of academic disciplines, should serve on every committee and should have input about the way that the assessment will be carried out. However, participation in the implementation process will not ensure faculty support of institutional efforts. For the implementation of institutional effectiveness to have the desired impact on the overall quality of the institution, faculty must know that the administration shares their commitment to assessment "as a tool for the improvement of teaching and learning" (Chandler, 1987, p. 5). Peter Ewell (1985), in a description of successful assessment programs, noted that model programs often have an explicit focus on the assessment and improvement of an individual degree program and that many programs fail because assessment and improvement are only undertaken at the institutional level.

The Study Group on the Conditions of Excellence in American Higher Education (1984) emphasized assessment as a means of feedback to improve teaching and learning. This group specifically recommended faculty involvement in the design and implementation of assessment programs for the following reason:

> The best way to connect assessment to improvement of teaching and learning is to insure that faculty have a proprietary interest in the assessment process . . . [as] such involvement will help faculty to specify—far more precisely than they do at present—the outcomes they expect from individual courses and academic programs. And the more precisely they can specify the outcomes, the more likely they are to match teaching approaches to those ends (p. 45).

Clearly, the faculty, as the specialists in their academic disciplines and as the direct link to students in the classroom, must be responsible for defining, revising, and judging the assessment of intended instructional outcomes. At the departmental level, outcomes must form a bridge between institutional goals for student learning/development and specific course and curriculum content. The educational outcomes must be broad enough to encompass the total curriculum yet concrete enough to have implications for changes in instructional methods and curriculum design. Therefore, faculty should limit the number of outcomes to be assessed to those that are meaningful at the departmental level and that are essential for the institution to accomplish its goals. Concentration on assessment of a few crucial outcomes is more productive than incomplete coverage of all departmental expectations.

As desired states of behavior, outcomes should focus on problem areas where improvements are needed and changes are expected. A continuation of the present conditions, although important, is not appropriate in an outcome statement. Thus, outcomes should be stated in terms of expected behaviors within a set time frame. Educational outcomes focus primarily on student behavior; however, faculty development can also be included since changes in faculty may have indirect effects on student learning.

How do departmental faculty begin the process of developing meaningful outcomes statements? A good resource is the manual *Developing Measurable Objectives* (1974), which contains a discussion of procedures for developing program goals and objectives. A beginning step is to complete a content analysis of current courses and curricula. A review of course syllabi and a study of the overall curriculum should be conducted. This curriculum review should not be limited to current local course offerings alone but should extend to other institutions that offer strong academic programs in the same field which the institution may wish to emulate.

In addition, faculty should consult other sources of information, including reports from national commissions and professional associations. Desirable outcomes of academic programs are often described in such reports. Then faculty can select those outcomes that are appropriate for their students as well as consistent with both the purpose of the institution and the objectives of the department.

To ensure that outcomes are aimed at appropriate levels of performance, faculty must know the achievement levels of the typical entering student in order to set the expected performance level of the typical exiting student. Outcomes frequently are statements of gains or changes that occur as a result of the college experience. Knowledge of high school preparation will assist in setting reasonable outcomes for first- and second-year college students. In some disciplines it is highly desirable to have placement test data not only to establish valid procedures for assigning students to remedial or advanced courses but also to describe skills and knowledge of the typical entering student. For upper-level undergraduate programs, faculty need to be familiar with prerequisite courses taught not only at their institution but at institutions from which students transfer.

A more difficult question is the expected level of performance for the exiting student, which should be stated in the educational outcomes. Within departments that primarily provide required courses at the freshman and sophomore levels contributing to the institution's general education requirements, outcomes may include the knowledge, skills, and attitudes judged necessary for success at upper-division levels. Do the expectations differ for those students who major in the discipline versus those who take only the introductory courses? Are the courses aimed at general skills that should continue to develop in other courses outside of the department?

For departments offering degrees, diplomas, or certificates, what outcomes are necessary for graduates to succeed in jobs or advanced academic programs? If the undergraduate degree provides the foundation for graduate or professional programs, faculty must be aware of the performance levels that institutions offering these programs expect of entering students. If the degree, diploma, or certificate is primarily aimed at preparing graduates for entry into jobs, then the outcomes must relate to job preparation and performance.

If a requirement for job entry is passing a licensing, certifying, or qualifying examination, then the knowledge and skills have already been defined, probably by a professional organization. In the absence of such examinations, faculty must work with other professionals to conduct job analyses of entry-level positions. A job analysis specifies the skills, knowledge, and behaviors necessary for the recent graduate to perform the job adequately.

Institutional goals in the educational area are not limited to development of "a depth of understanding in the major field and preprofessional programs preparing the graduate for employment" (Appendix A, p. 172). In the Expanded Statement of Institutional Purpose of the hypothetical institution, Our University, academic programs are to lay an "academic foundation in liberal studies in order to enhance students' communication and analytic skills, to provide an understanding of their intellectual and cultural heritage, and to assist them in the development of self-awareness, responsible leadership, and the capacity to make reasoned moral judgments" (Appendix A, p. 169). Thus, departments must address areas of social and personal development as well as cognitive development, which is usually the primary focus of curriculum objectives. Faculty must consider how their academic disciplines can contribute to social and personal development. For example, the study of foreign languages may contribute to students developing an interest in and tolerance of people from different cultures. The sociology, political science, and business management programs may focus on defining "responsible leadership" and having students judge the value of such leadership to our society.

Thus, outcomes should not be limited to the cognitive domain but should adequately cover the affective and skill areas. The classification of outcomes into these three areas—cognitive (knowledge), affective (attitudes), and skills (performance)—is helpful to ensure broad coverage of student changes. The cognitive domain, as described in Bloom's taxonomy of educational objectives (Bloom, 1956), includes knowledge, comprehension, application, analysis, synthesis, and evaluation. Faculty should specify the level of cognitive complexity required for students to demonstrate that learning has occurred. Is it sufficient for the student to pass an objective test that measures knowledge, or is the application of knowledge in simulation exercises a more appropriate measure?

The affective domain, described by Krathwohl and associates (1964), includes attitudes, beliefs, values, goals, and expectations which predispose a person to behave in certain ways. Affect or attitude must be directed toward a person, object, place, or idea. For example, to say that a student has a positive attitude is meaningless, but to add "toward writing" allows us to make some predictions about the student's behavior. We might expect the student to write more often, to write with observable pleasure, or to ask for help in writing.

Although such outcomes are generally not stated in course objectives, faculty also want to increase student interest in the subject matter—an affective outcome. Departments may be less inclined to state affective outcomes because of the problems associated with the measurement of attitudes. Henerson, Morris, and Fitz-Gibbon (1978, p. 13) have described those problems. First, it is impossible to measure attitudes directly; we must infer attitudes from behavior. Second, there may be inconsistency between attitudes and behavior; thus, more than one observation of behavior is essential in order to infer the attitude. Third, it is difficult to develop instruments that meet the accepted standards for reliability; attitudes do change, and stability in measuring them over time is often unattainable. Finally, because attitudes are constructs that cannot be directly observed, people disagree on the conceptual and operational definitions of specific attitudes.

Getting faculty to agree upon which attitudes are important for their students to develop is difficult enough, but getting them to agree upon the operational definitions of those attitudes—how they will be observed and measured—is even more difficult and may be the major stumbling block to setting affective outcomes. Perhaps more so than in the cognitive and skill areas, multiple measures that use different techniques (for example, interest inventories, interviews, and direct observation of behavior) are necessary for faculty to agree upon the outcomes and to draw conclusions from the assessment procedures.

Skills include, but are not limited to, psychomotor tasks that develop through imitation and practice. Physical education departments; the performing arts; professional programs like nursing, teaching, and dentistry; and technical, vocational, and trade programs all focus on skill development. Although knowledge of information may be a necessary condition to perform certain tasks, knowledge alone is not sufficient; practice is often the key to psychomotor performance. For example, the music department cannot adequately assess the aspiring pianist through an objective test that measures recognition of musical notes, time, and rhythmic patterns. Actual performance of several pieces in which a student demonstrates the ability to read music, using correct time and rhythms, is necessary to determine the student's level of proficiency.

In addition to psychomotor skills, general skills expected of all students are usually identified. The Expanded Statement of Institutional Purpose for Our University explicitly states five general skills that all students should master before exiting the institution. Our University's students are expected to

1. Express themselves clearly, correctly, and succinctly in a written manner;
2. Make an effective verbal presentation of their ideas concerning a topic;
3. Read and offer an analysis of periodical literature concerning a topic of interest;
4. Complete accurately basic mathematical calculations;
5. Demonstrate a sufficient level of computer literacy.

These skills are usually addressed in the general education component of the curriculum, which crosses academic departments. Reading, writing, speaking, mathematical computation, and computer literacy may be directly related to specific courses; however, the skills should continue to develop across the entire curriculum. For example, students may be required to take a speech course which will provide them with fundamental skills in developing an idea and presenting it orally. However, students should use these skills in many other courses, through class discussions if not formal oral presentations. Although the speech department should accept more responsibility for this skill, all academic departments should provide both practice and feedback to their students.

Who should be responsible for setting the educational outcomes for general education? This is a question that each institution must address, for it also implies responsibility for assessing these skills. Perhaps, as with our hypothetical institution, these should be institutionwide outcomes, set by a faculty committee that broadly represents the academic community. This approach supports the notion of shared responsibility for the development of general education skills. The task confronting each department is to determine how its courses and programs foster development of the skills.

The academic department then has responsibility for reviewing its courses and programs, examining the professional literature, and collaborating with colleagues from other institutions—including high schools, two-year colleges, four-year colleges, institutions with professional and graduate programs, and employers—to determine desirable outcomes for its students. In addition to student outcomes, however, outcomes for faculty development may also be addressed. Such outcomes may address improved teaching through involvement in professional meetings where the latest findings in their disciplines are discussed, presentation and publication of original research, and participation in workshops designed to enhance teaching effectiveness.

Research and Public Service Outcomes

Most four-year institutions incorporate references to research, teaching, and public service in their mission statements. Although two-year institutions may not include research, their teaching and public service missions are usually very apparent.

The establishment of outcomes in these areas may flow logically from the mission statement. If they do not, efforts by external organizations to develop standards or statements of recommended professional practice, research, and public service may serve as sources for establishing administrative objectives. In this regard, the trend toward self-regulation on the part of individual and institutionally based professional membership associations, combined with increased interest in the evaluation of such services and programs, has led to the emergence of a growing, but somewhat fugitive, literature base on the evaluation of noninstructional areas.

In the area of research services, the identification of outcomes employed in measuring institutional effectiveness may have several sources. First, and most common, is the specification of direct measures of research program activity. Here, the number and dollar amounts of proposals developed, submitted, and funded often serve as the primary reference point. Such data are usually collected in a routine manner because they are frequently required by state and federal agencies for reporting purposes. Baseline external funding statistics are often used as benchmarks for formulating intended research outcomes.

Beyond the usual quantitative outcome indicators, attitudinal indicators gathered primarily through satisfaction surveys of the users of a sponsored program or research services office are helpful in formulating outcome indicators. The most common focus of such surveys would be feedback regarding the scope of desired services coupled with measures of satisfaction with existing services.

Information obtained from a management audit may also be helpful in formulating outcomes related to an assessment of research services. The primary focus in this regard is on the efficiency of procedures employed in administering contracts and grants. Such procedures are generally designed to assure the orderly commitment of external and internal funds in administering contracts for special projects and programs. Audits may be performed by a team of state auditors or by independent accounting firms.

Often the administration of grants and contracts will be carried out by an institution's business office, whereas assistance in obtaining research funds and services is provided to faculty from an office reporting to academic affairs or the graduate school. In the former instance, familiarity with contract and grant procedures developed by the National Association of College and University Business Officers (NACUBO) (1987) may be helpful. In the latter instance, information concerning desired research services and information sources useful in obtaining grants and contracts is available through the activities and information networks of such professional organizations as the National Council of University Research Administrators (NCURA) or the Society of Research Administrators (SRA).

In the area of public service, continuing education professionals have focused considerable attention upon the definition of standards and the formulation of principles of good practice. The Principles of Good Practice for Continuing Education (Council on the Continuing Education Unit, 1984) are designed to serve sponsors, providers, and users of continuing education in collegiate and noncollegiate settings. Development of more current standards for continuing education was preceded by a study of attitudes toward previously existing standards of good practice in a variety of organizational settings (House, 1983).

The 18 general principles and 70 statements of good practice in relation to learning needs, learning outcomes, learning experiences, assessment, and administration of continuing education programs may serve as a model for research, public service, or other units of various types.

Educational Support Services

Educational support services are equivalent to "Academic Support Services" in the example Expanded Statement of Institutional Purpose in Appendix A of this *Handbook*. Collier (1978) defined academic support services as ". . .those activities carried out in direct support of one or more of the three primary programs (Instruction, Research, Public Service)" (p. 37). Subprograms or areas of academic support include library services, museums and galleries, educational media services, academic computing support, academic administration and personnel development, and course and curriculum development.

There may not be universal agreement when one attempts to define the administrative areas included under a given functional area. The broader Program Classification Structure (PCS), described by Myers and Topping (1974), helps to define administrative units falling under the primary PCS areas of instruction, research, public service, academic support, student service, and instructional support.

Because of the nature of these programs, educational support services must coordinate closely with instructional programs in the development of their respective goals, objectives, and assessment procedures. This is particularly true of personnel development and course and curriculum development. The objectives in these particular areas will, in most instances, be developed by the same academic departments or schools that are developing the student outcomes, goals and objectives. For example, a department that has an educational outcome of improving student computer skills might also have a faculty development objective related to improving faculty computer-related skills to improve teaching effectiveness in that particular area. As another example, a psychology department might find, through evaluation of student outcomes assessments, that majors are weak in the areas of perception and physiological psychology as measured by the GRE or another end-of-program test. Consequently, that department might develop objectives and assessment procedures related to improving the courses in those areas or to developing courses not currently included in the curriculum.

Other areas such as library services and computing services are independent units. These units in particular must coordinate their objectives with those of the academic units, which, in turn, should coordinate their plans with the support service units to be sure that intended outcomes requiring substantial increases in resources or services are feasible. For example, the library may have an objective of automating its catalog and providing an on-line catalog search service to all departments. If the departments are not aware of this intention and have not requested funds for appropriate equipment in their budgets, this objective will not be achieved in its entirety. Automating the catalog can be achieved by the library without support from other units, but the use of an on-line service by academic units depends upon the purchase of equipment out of departmental budgets. Unless academic units allocate funds for equipment, the service will very likely be unused.

The assessment procedures developed by academic support units may differ from those developed by academic units in that examination of records, logs of activities, and supporting documents for annual reports may play a much larger role. A library can document that its catalog is automated by reporting details of the development procedure and having the catalog available for review. An art museum can document that it has increased its collection in a particular area by listing new acquisitions in a simple report, assuming that dated sales agreements or letters describing donations are on file and assuming that the new acquisitions are available for examination. In summary, academic support units will most often be documenting activities using routine record keeping and reports and will rarely have to use special data collection methods or surveys.

Establishment of Administrative Objectives in Nonacademic Units

In the area of setting objectives for administrative services, the work of Wergin and Braskamp (1987) is particularly helpful, as are the self-regulatory efforts of the Council for the Advancement of Standards for Student Services/Development Programs (1986) and the Student Services Program Review Project (1986), which developed standards of professional practice and evaluation approaches in a number of nonacademic areas.

The Council for the Advancement of Standards (CAS) has developed a set of evaluation standards and guidelines for evaluating sixteen functional administrative areas. The work of CAS was carried out over a 6-year period through the efforts of 22 CAS professional associations with support and encouragement from the American Council on Education's Advisory Committee on Self-Regulation Initiatives and the Council on Postsecondary Accreditation (COPA).

In the development of the CAS standards and guidelines, no particular organizational or administrative structure was presupposed or mandated. Therefore, the standards that emerged apply to all types of postsecondary institutions. General standards were developed for each of the following functional areas: mission, program, leadership and management, organization and administration, human resources, funding, facilities, legal responsibilities, equal opportunity, access and affirmative action, campus and community relations, multicultural programs and services, ethics, and evaluation.

Academic support services for which CAS standards were developed include academic advising, learning assistance programs, faculty development programs, and computing services. Student service areas addressed in the CAS standards and guidelines include career planning and placement, college unions, commuter student services, disabled student services, fraternities and sororities, housing and residence life, judicial programs, minority student services, recreational sports, religious programs, student activities, and orientation programs. In the area of institutional support services, CAS standards and guidelines were proposed for the evaluation of research and evaluation services.

The Student Services Program Review Project (SSPRP), developed in California, is of particular interest to the community college sector but has general applicability to all postsecondary institutions. The goal of the project was to develop and pilot test evaluation designs in order to assist colleges in implementing program evaluations for selected campus-based student services programs. Over a 3-year period, more than a thousand persons were involved in the development and testing of evaluation designs—including goals, criteria, measures, and methods—that were field based and field produced. The following were the specific objectives (SSPRP, 1986, p. 3):

1. Develop evaluation models.
2. Develop data collection, data analysis, and information-reporting procedures.
3. Pilot test evaluation models and procedures.
4. Widely disseminate models and procedures.

5. Develop support materials and services to assist colleges in implementing program evaluations appropriate to their institutions.

The SSPRP project developed evaluation designs and procedures for admissions and records, assessment services, career/life planning, counseling, financial aid, job placement, student affairs, and tutorial services.

Rather than focusing upon existing generalized program evaluation models and their applicability to administrative settings, Wergin and Braskamp (1987) have discussed issues and strategies for evaluating specific programs. They presented specific criteria and evaluative schema for institutional planning, business affairs, intercollegiate athletic programs, student support services, counseling centers, faculty development programs, and campus computing services. Key questions addressed are as follows: (1) How can institutional researchers and academic administrators authorize and produce information on program effectiveness that is useful for decision making? and (2) How are administrators to know how well these administrative and support services are working and what might be done to improve them?

Summary

Institutions can expect a considerable degree of variance in the technical merit of statements of departmental/program intended outcomes/objectives. Particularly at the inception of institutional effectiveness operations, such differences are not only acceptable but desirable to the extent that they reflect active involvement by the institution's departments. However, this resource section and the examples contained in Appendix B suggest that outcomes/objectives should be linked to the Expanded Statement of Institutional Purpose; should exhibit many of the attributes described earlier; and in most cases should be measurable.

References: Cited and Recommended

The reference list for both of the resource sections accompanying Chapter 4 is provided at the end of the section entitled "Designing the Assessment Process." Refer to pages 136–138.

Designing the
Assessment Process

Linda Pratt, Donald Reichard, Brenda Rogers

Linkage of Assessment Results through Outcomes and Objectives to Statement of Purpose

Linkage of each unit's statements of intentions (outcomes or objectives) to the institution's expanded statement of purpose and the appropriateness of specific assessment procedures are among the most important factors in designing a campuswide assessment process. The *Resource Manual on Institutional Effectiveness* published by the Commission on Colleges of the Southern Association of Colleges and Schools (1987) contains a suggested format for development of outcomes/objectives at the unit level which ensures that linkage is maintained between the institution's statement of purpose and the unit objectives. The examples in Appendix B are depictions of another format and include an appropriate excerpt from the statement of purpose before intended departmental/program outcomes/objectives are stated. Assessment criteria and procedures are then described. Regardless of the format utilized, if the assessment results are consistent with the intended outcomes/objectives and the linkage with the institution's statement of purpose is assured, then solid evidence is provided concerning accomplishment of institutional-level intentions.

Selection of Measures: The Process

The selection of measures at the unit level is a highly individual process, particularly in the administrative and support areas. In those areas, a general philosophy rather than a specific process may be more appropriate. In general, this philosophy might be defined as using the simplest and the most straightforward assessment procedure possible. This means making extensive use of files, logs of activities, and summaries included in annual reports. Only when the regular reporting structure is inadequate or when there is an indication of special problems in an area should special procedures such as external reviews, surveys, and other special or unusual data collection techniques be considered. In assessment of student outcomes, however, the data may not exist, making new approaches necessary. Once the desired outcomes are defined, each department, school, and institutionwide program, such as the general studies program, should carefully review both standardized and locally developed assessment procedures to select those relevant to the stated outcomes. The faculty of the departments and schools should be involved in this selection process, with the offices responsible for institutional research and testing providing technical assistance in selection and administration of the instruments and in analysis of the results.

Assessment of Knowledge and General Skills

After the faculty have agreed upon departmental outcomes, they must then take part in selection or development of methods for assessing progress toward these outcomes. Assessment instruments are available not only from testing companies but also from individuals who have developed instruments for research purposes. A thorough review of existing instruments includes an evaluation of the following:

1. The appropriateness of the instrument for the target population
2. The reliability of scores
3. The validity of the scores for the intended use
4. The normative data to assist in interpreting the scores

Published Resources

Several resources will be helpful in the search for published tests. *Tests in Print III: An Index to Tests, Test Reviews, and the Literature of Specific Tests* (Mitchell, 1983) contains a comprehensive list of commercial tests printed in the English language. The *Mental Measurement Yearbook* series contains reviews of tests as well as factual information about the author, publisher, publication date, cost, administrative time, and grade levels for which the tests are appropriate. Instruments published after 1972 are reviewed in the ninth edition (Mitchell, 1985). However, tests published prior to 1972 may also be contained in the recent edition of the *Yearbook* if new versions of the test have been released or new information is available on the tests.

With a grant from the Fund for the Improvement of Postsecondary Education, the University of Tennessee at Knoxville has developed the *Bibliography of Assessment Instruments* for colleges and universities, as referred to in the resource section entitled "Cognitive Assessment Instruments: Availability and Utilization." This bibliography includes tests used to assess affective and cognitive changes in students and provides descriptive information about the purpose, publisher and address, target audience, cost, scoring procedures, and administrative time. Complimentary copies of this publication are available from

Dr. Trudy Banta
The Assessment Resource Center
The University of Tennessee at Knoxville
2046 Terrace Avenue
Knoxville, TN 37996–3504
Telephone: (615) 974–0883

The separate resource sections at the end of Chapter 3 include discussions of specific instruments used to assess cognitive and attitudinal changes. Further information on the validity and reliability of the ACT COMP tests is included in *Defining and Measuring General Education Knowledge and Skill* (Forrest & Steele, 1982). And, although the Undergraduate Assessment Program has been discontinued as an operational program, the Educational Testing Service allows institutions to rent the business field test. Designed for undergraduates who have completed business programs, the test covers accounting, economics, quantitative business analysis, finance, marketing, management, and business law. Only local scoring is available.

Beyond the previously cited attitudinal instruments, UCLA's Robert Pace (1983) has developed the well-known College Student Experiences Questionnaire (CSEQ). This is a self-report instrument measuring student involvement in 16 college activities, 21 areas in which students estimate gains as a result of attending college, and 7 dimensions of the college environment. Comparative data are available for participating institutions. The CSEQ is used to assess student behaviors such as the percentage of students using the library or various student services. Thus, it may be particularly helpful in establishing baseline measurements for a range of activities which may be helpful in setting institutional or subunit goals. Although the research is promising, the primary application of research findings thus far appears to be at the institutional rather than the departmental level.

Unpublished Resources

Individual researchers also have developed noncommercially available measures of psychological and educational constructs which are reported in the research literature. One resource cited by Anastasi (1988) for identifying these unpublished instruments is *Tests in Microfiche*, available from Test Collection, ETS. Often these questionnaires and scales are available free of charge simply by contacting the researcher. In their *Directory of Unpublished Experimental Mental Measures: Volume IV*, Goldman and Osborne (1985) listed a number of experimental test instruments (i.e., tests that are not currently marketed commercially). This volume serves as a reference enabling the reader to identify potentially useful measures and sources from which technical information concerning the instruments can be obtained. The validity of all such instruments for program evaluation may not be established, so an initial step may be validation of the instruments for their intended use.

Other Assessment Methods

If a review of the literature and published instruments yields no tests or surveys appropriate for evaluation of departmental outcomes, then the faculty must devise their own assessment means. The search for appropriate measures, however, should not be limited to tests and questionnaires. Observations of behavior, interviews, and unobtrusive measures (Terenzini, 1987) offer alternatives. Performance measures, such as writing a paper, delivering a speech, or using a computer to solve a problem, are appropriate for many general education and psychomotor skills. In fact, performance measures may be more relevant to the instructional methods and intended outcomes than multiple-choice questions.

Interviewing students is another way to collect evaluation data. Questions must be standardized, interviewers should be trained, individually administered interviews must be conducted, and the responses must be analyzed—all of which are time-consuming activities. However, the process may yield a wealth of qualitative data regarding students'perceptions, expectations, and values. If faculty or advisors conduct the interviews, an unintended outcome may be an increase in meaningful dialogue between students and faculty/advisors. A study of changes in students over their 4 years at Stanford University, *Careerism and Intellectualism among College Students* (Katchadourian & Boli, 1985), illustrated the use of the interview method to collect data on undergraduates.

Examples of unobtrusive measures are records of student use of facilities and services and student attendance. For example, professors often place supplemental reading material on reserve in the library. Frequency of use is an indicator of the interest of students in the subject. Such "counts" of student behavior may be good indicators of attitudes.

Another approach is the use of an external examiner, as proposed by Bobby Fong (1987) at the American Association for Higher Education Assessment Forum. He suggested that an outside expert in the academic field can be an "effective way to assess both student learning and curricular coherence in a major," which can lead to "valuable information and recommendations as to where curricular requirements need to be more specific and how course offerings need to be strengthened" (p. 17). The outside consultant could be asked to address the outcomes specified by the departments and to critique the curriculum.

Before extensive data collection is undertaken, sources of existing data should be identified. Most institutions maintain computerized files with historical data on students, faculty, and staff. A wealth of information about retention, enrollment and graduation trends, grades, and course-taking patterns is available from student information systems. Computerized files and report programs may have to be designed to answer important questions—for example, on the average, how long does it take for an undergraduate to complete a baccalaureate degree? However, the data are available without new collection efforts. Peter Ewell (1987) has described the basic principles in building cohort files and conducting retention studies from data maintained on college campuses, and a resource section in Chapter 3 contains further details on this subject.

To assist in the evaluation of departmental outcomes, computerized reports must include separate analyses for each department.

Assuming that a fourth-generation language, like SAS (1985), is used to build the files and generate the reports, a programmer can slightly modify the standard report to produce departmental reports. Coordination with the institutional research office or administrative data processing is essential to ensure that reports, like retention studies, answer questions at the departmental level.

Routine reports required by the governing board, state agencies, the federal government, and professional accrediting agencies offer additional sources of information. The IPEDS (formerly HEGIS) reports required by the federal government are useful if the data are analyzed over several years to identify trends in enrollment and graduation. The Institutional Research Office should be able to identify the standard reports that may help departments with assessment.

Locally Developed Tests and Surveys

The development of tests and attitudinal surveys is a time-consuming task requiring much expertise in the field of tests and measurement. Departments that choose to develop their own achievement tests will likely need assistance from testing experts. Testing companies will work with institutions in the development of instruments. As indicated in the resource section on cognitive instruments, some institutions committed to outcomes assessment have established their own assessment centers, staffed with experts to assist departments in the process of setting outcomes and selecting or developing appropriate measures. Most institutions will be hard pressed to justify such an expenditure without specific external funding.

Although focusing on elementary and secondary education, Morris and Fitz-Gibbon (1978) described the general process for measuring achievement as part of a program evaluation. To construct a departmental achievement test, faculty must carefully state the outcomes/ objectives to be covered in the test. The objectives should include specification of both the content and the cognitive processes. Test items are then constructed to measure the outcomes/objectives, with the item format carefully chosen to require the cognitive processes specified by the objectives. Items and the reliability of the instrument should be analyzed. Finally, validity of the scores for the intended use should be examined. Although many excellent references describe the process of developing achievement tests, it is not a simple task. However, in those instances where no existing achievement test adequately covers the program outcomes/objectives, the only alternative is the development of departmental examinations.

Attitudinal surveys are generally easier to construct than achievement tests. The key is to develop items to which students will respond truthfully and which relate to the intended outcomes. ACT has an item bank of attitudinal items from which institutions can select those relevant to their needs. Existing surveys should be examined for examples of the types of questions and response formats. After the questionnaire is constructed, it should be reviewed by experts for their suggestions and then pretested with students.

Review of Assessment Means Available for Research and Service Outcomes and Administrative Objectives

A wide range of resources may be employed in setting research and public service outcomes and administrative objectives. One of the most helpful general references is the *Outcomes Measures and Procedures Manual* (Micek, Service, & Lee, 1975). This document specifies possible measures that administrators might wish to employ, as well as definitions, data sources, and procedures for collecting such measures. The previous section on identifying research and public service outcomes and administrative objectives emphasized the self-regulatory influence of professional associations in setting standards and guidelines for good professional practice. Other means of assessing outcomes and setting administrative objectives include the use of direct measures, attitudinal measures, and data system indicators.

Direct Measures

Direct measures of program outcomes are often implicit in a program's operational activities. In the area of sponsored research, this may include information concerning the number of research proposals formulated, the number of proposals submitted, the requested levels of funding by organizational subunit or discipline, the duration of proposed funding activity, as well as the actual level and duration of funded activity by subunit. Goals identified in the Expanded Statement of Institutional Purpose may also be stated and analyzed in terms of the sources of restricted revenue (federal, state, or local governments, or private gifts and contracts) from which sponsored research moneys were sought and obtained.

Public service/community impact measures that institutions may wish to consider include (a) enrollment levels/community participation in program offerings; (b) the extent to which an institution participates in community affairs or makes its social, cultural, and recreational programs and facilities available to the community; or (c) the economic impact of an institution upon its local community.

Attitudinal Measures

Several types of surveys may be helpful in the assessment of progress in reaching program outcomes and objectives in the sponsored research and community service areas. The first type of attitudinal measure may be a needs survey seeking input from faculty, students, or community clientele about the services or educational programs that are needed most. Once services and programs have been implemented in response to defined needs, user surveys may be quite helpful in assessing the degree of satisfaction and eliciting suggestions for the improvement of existing or expanded programs and services. Longitudinal follow-up studies of program participants may be helpful in assessing the long-term effects of an institution's program and service offerings. All too often, institutions survey only the clientele whom they are currently serving. Efforts must also be made to obtain reactions from persons who express interest in program offerings but do not actually participate in an institution's activities. Such surveys may help identify obstacles to program participation that may be remedied in the future.

Data System Indicators

In the research and public service areas, as in most areas of institutional operations, the institution's normal operations may provide a range of data system indicators useful in assessing outcomes and progress toward stated administrative objectives. Normal federal data-reporting procedures will yield financial data on research and public service activities via the IPEDS Financial Statistics Report. Often, additional reports required at the state level will also yield standard indicators of the extent of sponsored program or public service activities. The National Science Foundation (NSF) surveys, as well as survey responses to a number of collegiate guides at the graduate and undergraduate levels, may also provide a variety of outcomes indicators. Virtually every administrative unit will file an annual report with the office to which it reports. Information in these reports may provide a starting point in assessing progress toward goals and objectives. In short, if an office maintains any type of database on a central administrative computer or a microcomputer, it has the capability of transforming its operational data into analytical information suitable for evaluating program and administrative objectives.

Assessment Means Particularly Appropriate for Two-Year Institutions

Two-year institutions have unique missions requiring slightly different assessment procedures. Although much of the foregoing will apply to two-year institutions, some outcomes are unique. For example, community and junior colleges usually have the mission of providing the first two years of college to enable students to transfer to senior institutions. Thus, transfer student graduation rates from four-year institutions offer an excellent measure of the overall success of the two-year college. However, at the departmental level, meaningful outcomes are the transferability of credits earned in the department and the performance of students in upper-division courses.

Links between Two-Year and Four-Year Institutions

Senior institutions should provide important outcomes information on the transferability of credit hours, grades earned by transfers in upper-division courses, cumulative grade-point averages, and the academic standing of transfers after one year at the four-year institution. Although senior institutions cannot publicly release data concerning individuals without their permission, these institutions may have the technical capability to provide summary statistics of transfer student performance and should seek legal counsel concerning their ability to release data to two-year institutions concerning individual students.

In North Carolina, four-year institutions have been authorized to feed back information to two-year colleges for research purposes, so long as precautions have been taken to protect the identity of students from inadvertent public release. This feedback system is coordinated by the General Administration of the University of North Carolina System. The 16 public universities provide files on transfer student performance to General Administration. From these files, the system office generates annual reports with the average performance data for each institution from which sufficient numbers of students transferred in any given year. Thus, all 58 community and technical colleges, as well as the private two-year colleges, receive information on the performance of their students who transferred to the public universities. Without such state- or system-level coordination, senior institutions might be reluctant to fulfill separate requests from many different two-year institutions. Thus, coordination of the reporting process at the state or system level may be necessary for two-year institutions to receive reliable information on their graduates' performance at senior institutions.

Assessing Educational Outcomes

The following educational outcome addresses the performance of two-year transfer students at senior institutions from the English department's perspective:

> The expected outcome is that graduates who complete the college transfer program will transfer sufficient hours of credit to satisfy all of the general education requirements in English at senior institutions. The assessment procedures are surveys of the major state institutions to which our students transfer, to be conducted every 3 years to determine the transferability of English hours. If English courses are not accepted for transfer, then the courses will be revised to reflect the content of lower-level English courses at the major senior institutions.

Community and technical colleges have occupational programs specifically aimed at preparing students for entry-level jobs. Programs are developed in response to the employment needs and opportunities in the geographic region served by the college. Measures of the success of the occupational programs are their graduates' ability to obtain entry-level jobs, job performance, and starting salaries. Satisfaction of both the graduates and employers with the occupational preparation is an affective outcome that should be addressed; for example:

> Major employers of engineering technicians in the county will be surveyed every 3 years to determine their satisfaction with the preparation of our institution's graduates, the demand for engineering technicians, and the level of skill and knowledge expected of entry-level employees. The engineering technician programs will be reviewed in light of the feedback from employers.

One central mission of comprehensive community colleges involves adult basic education. Achievement tests specifically designed for adult education programs, like the Adult Basic Learning Examination (ABLE), should be used to assess progress. Conducting follow-up studies of adults who complete adult education courses is another method of evaluating such outcomes as satisfaction with basic literacy courses. Other less direct measures—but ones that may be more critical from a societal perspective—are job attainment and further education or training completed.

Comprehensive community colleges also address the mission of preparing students for the Tests of General Educational Development (GED), the high school equivalency examinations. Passing rates on the GED tests are measures of the success of such programs.

Comprehensive community colleges also offer remedial programs as a part of their mission. Frequently referred to as developmental education, the remedial programs attempt to prepare students for college-level work. The evaluation of remedial programs poses many challenges. How realistic is the expectation that high school graduates lacking in basic educational skills will make sufficient progress in a quarter, a year, or even 2 years to enable them to succeed in college? Although future success in college is the ultimate goal, intermediate goals may be more appropriate for remedial programs. For example, progress may be measured by improvement after instruction in reading, writing, and mathematical skills, based upon comparisons of pretest and posttest scores. Caution needs to be exercised, however, in the selection or development of tests for the purpose of comparing these scores. The test should be at the appropriate skill level so that gains are real and not artifacts due to regression toward the mean. Pascarella (1987) offers a lucid discussion of the pros and cons of value-added approaches to assessment, which have direct implications for the assessment of remedial education.

Importance of Multiple Assessment Procedures for Each Outcome/Objective

In any area of research the reliability of the results depends in part on the various procedures used to collect the data and in part on the appropriateness of the particular measure chosen. As in other research endeavors, the reliability of the results can be improved by the use of multiple measures. Although the term *multiple measures* is generally interpreted to mean two or more different measures of the same effect, it can also mean repeating the same measure at different intervals or, more rarely, having more than one observer measure the same effect at a single point in time.

Some outcomes are stated in such a way that a single measure will provide appropriate information for assessment of that objective. For example, Our University has a goal to "increase the level of organized or sponsored research expenditures by 5% per year for the next 5 years." An audit report indicating the increase in expenditures each year would be a single measure adequate to assess that goal. On the other hand, the goal to "study the university's general education program to determine whether revisions are desirable" would probably require more than one outcome/objective measure for adequate assessment. Some type of test or examination measuring student achievement might be paired with measures of student success in subsequent upper-level courses, examination of course syllabi to determine if course content is consistent with the goals of the program, and possibly a review of the program by an outside group or individual. A third goal, to "give increased emphasis to recruitment of minority students (i.e., Hispanic, Black, Asian, and Native American) and increase their representation in the overall student population" might best be assessed by establishing a base of the number and percentage of students in each racial/ethnic category and monitoring changes in both number and percentage over a period of several years. In this case, repeated measures of the same data element constitute the most appropriate method of assessment.

In summary, as in selecting the specific method of assessment, the determination of the number of different methods of assessment or the number of times each measure needs to be repeated to establish trend data is a decision that must be made based on the content of the goal or objective.

Designing the Assessment Process

Focusing the Assessment Effort

The primary focus in implementing institutional effectiveness is by definition at the institutional level. The linkage of academic and administrative outcomes and objectives to an enhanced statement of purpose is necessary to assure that subunits are carrying out institutionwide missions. The essence of top-down linkage is to demonstrate that subunit goals and objectives support the broader mission statement. On the other hand, with bottom-up linkage, statements of purpose emerge and are revised as the outcomes and objectives of schools, divisions, or departments are altered. If statements of purpose are the sum of the institution's parts, institutions must take care to examine the extent to which such statements may need to be revised in order to reflect what is occurring within various operational units. The need to reconcile intentions and actions assumes that statements of purpose, goals, objectives, and outcome statements are continuously being reviewed. If careful analysis of subunit outcomes/objectives suggests that various clusters do not reflect the existing statement of purpose, development of a revised statement of purpose is probably in order.

Progressive Revision of Standards

As missions, goals, objectives, and outcomes are reviewed on a continuous basis, the standards by which their achievement is measured also need to be reconsidered on a periodic basis. If, for example, the percentage of students successfully passing board exams in nursing increased at the rate of 2% per year over a 3-year period, it might be logical to consider adopting statements of intentions that would require progressively higher percentages of students to pass such exams. Judgment will play a crucial role in determining realistic performance standards.

Design of Feedback Mechanisms

Based on the assessment of outcomes and objectives, reports for presentation to academic and administrative departments should be prepared. Mechanisms for providing feedback from the evaluation should include written documents, probably in the form of a report addressing each of the stated outcomes/objectives as well as tabular data. Although narrative descriptions of the findings are suggested, graphic presentations are usually more effective. An objective of the assessment process might be to summarize the data for each outcome/objective on one page through either a table or graph with a short explanatory paragraph highlighting the major findings.

Faculty and staff committees may be involved in analyzing and reporting the information that is disseminated to the entire department for review. Time for faculty and staff to discuss the report and to offer their interpretation of the results is essential. Rather than discussing the results at a regular departmental meeting, the chair or director may identify at the beginning of the academic year the date of a special meeting for the interpretation of the assessment findings. A retreat or workshop may be the best mechanism for communicating how well the department met its objectives. Combining oral presentations with supporting visual materials can effectively draw attention to the data.

Interpretation of the data requires comparison of the results to norms or expectations, depending on how the standards are established. When outcomes are stated as desired states, then comparisons of obtained results with desired outcomes may be effective in focusing on strengths and weaknesses. If standardized instruments are used, comparison of the department's performance with an appropriate normative sample aids in interpretation of the results. If an institutionwide survey is conducted, the department can be compared to the institution as a whole or to some subgroup, such as a division, college, or school. At the very least, the same data should be collected over a period of time to show progress toward goals. Line graphs clearly illustrate trends over time and identify progress toward goals.

After the results have been interpreted, faculty and staff should focus on the implications for changes in courses, curriculum, instructional methods, faculty development, advising, and other areas. Also, the assessment findings must be communicated to an institutionwide committee that has responsibility for the evaluation of institutional effectiveness. Processing assessment results through a centralized clearinghouse will facilitate the usage of results for institutional improvement.

Peter Ewell (1984) cited three examples of "self-regarding institutions" that engage in a continuous assessment process and use assessment results for curriculum and institutional improvement. Alverno College, Northeast Missouri State University (NMSU), and the University of Tennessee at Knoxville (UTK) differ in their approaches to assessment as well as in their motivation for carrying out assessments. However, both NMSU and UTK link the results of assessment to budgeting processes. NMSU uses the results in its budget requests to the state. UTK is responding to the Tennessee Higher Education Commission's "performance funding" program, which distributes additional state money based on measures of student outcomes and program evaluations.

Given Ewell's analysis of effective assessment programs in postsecondary institutions, we conclude that the review of departmental outcomes must be incorporated into the regular resource-allocation and budget-planning processes in order to be effective in promoting institutional change. The linkage of departmental evaluations to institutional-level assessment is most effectively accomplished through the planning and budgeting processes. Departmental requests for budgets could be presented to an institutionwide committee which reviews progress toward last year's goals and objectives and determines resource needs to support the proposed objectives.

If the departmental evaluations result in increases or decreases in budgets to support change and improvement, then faculty and staff will view the process as more than a mere exercise. The tangible ramifications of the evaluation process will lead to serious efforts to demonstrate departmental outcomes, although a tendency to set aspirations or intentions that are easily attained and/or to lower standards over time may be observed in some departments. Therefore, an institutional committee should carefully review the revised outcomes and objectives to ensure that criteria and standards are appropriate.

The institutional review will result in revisions of outcomes and objectives in light of institutional goals and resource availability. The committee and department heads can negotiate the outcomes and objectives for the next cycle to ensure compatibility with institutional purposes and goals and feasibility given available resources.

At the departmental level, the reports of assessment findings are reviewed, discussed, and revised by members of the department. After discussions with the institutional committee, the director or department chair/head can agree to certain revisions in objectives. Finally, the director or department chair could communicate these changes to the faculty and staff. Resource allocations would be directly linked to the proposed objectives and to the departmental strengths and weaknesses identified in the evaluation reports.

The Logistical Support of Assessment

Assessment can be a costly process, in terms of both money and human resources. Throughout this chapter the authors have encouraged the use of simple assessment procedures. Both academic and administrative units have repeatedly been encouraged to use existing data wherever possible, to minimize the use of special reports, and to use special instruments and surveys sparingly; however, even the most carefully designed process will require extra expenditures and added effort on the part of faculty, administrators, and staff.

Student outcomes assessment is one area in which additional expense is almost unavoidable. Although attitude assessment instruments are relatively inexpensive, the total cost of administering a survey can be quite high. The costs of an initial mailing, return postage, and the mailing of one or more follow-up postcards must be considered as well. A simple alumni survey of a graduating class of 1,000 could cost well over $1,000, depending on the particular survey and the method of scoring and analysis. Academic assessment instruments are even more costly. Freshman placement testing can be less expensive, provided instruments are scored on campus, but even this is a major expenditure. A decision to purchase commercially available surveys or services rather than invest one's own staff resources ends up as a trade-off requiring judgment as to which resource is most limited.

Each campus should review the assessments planned—particularly those that require student testing or surveying of campus or outside groups—to determine whether the needs of several units can be met by a coordinated effort. In many cases, a single survey can meet the needs of several administrative units as well as the needs of several academic departments or schools. Where this is possible, the time and effort to prepare, administer, and score the instrument as well as the actual costs of mailing and follow-up can be greatly reduced. As an added benefit, the return rate is likely to be higher if the same individuals do not receive multiple instruments from different units within the college or university.

As the assessment procedures are being developed and identified, campus planning groups should be identifying sources of funds to be used for assessment. The success of a student outcomes assessment process will depend, in large part, on whether assessment can become a regular budget item. If new sources of funds must be identified each year, the process will eventually die as other priorities intervene. It is also important for some person or group to be given responsibility for carrying out those parts of the assessment that are coordinated and for that individual (or group) to be given the time and resources to complete the tasks on an ongoing basis.

As the assessment process progresses, a large body of data concerning the students and the operations of the university will accumulate. At this point, two questions arise: (1) How will the information be stored or maintained? and (2) Who will have access to what data? Each campus will need to determine, for each type of information, who is to have access and who is to maintain that data. The campuses will then need to identify an office that will be responsible for maintaining a consolidated list of information sources, a library of reports, and documented computer files of survey and student academic assessment data. Following the campus determination of access, that office would serve as a clearinghouse for assessment data. Most information would be available in either raw data or report form. Some information, such as that included in detailed annual reports, might be available only in the offices generating the reports and the files of supervisors receiving the reports. However, even in those cases, the clearinghouse would maintain copies of unit outcomes/objectives reports indicating which assessments are appropriate and the current assessment results relating to each.

As indicated by this discussion, a major assessment program— even one carefully planned to decentralize and simplify the procedure—requires a major commitment on the part of the institution. This commitment must take the form of providing resources as a part of the regular budget and of assigning responsibility for overall coordination to a single office or individual.

Summary

It would be a mistake to picture the design of the assessment process in a manner similar to the blueprint analogy utilized by Yost in a preceding resource section concerning the development of the Expanded Statement of Institutional Purpose, because the assessment process must by its design be reactive in nature. Rather, those charged with responsibility for coordination of assessment activities must gather the best materials available, apply these assessment materials to the blueprint provided by intended outcomes/objectives, assist in development of new materials to fill the gaps in assessment coverage, seek to make the application of various assessment methodologies across the campus as efficient as possible, and feed back the information to the various levels of the institutions as effectively as possible.

References: Cited and Recommended

American College Testing Program. (1987). *College outcomes measures program, 1987–88*. Iowa City, IA: Author.
Anastasi, A. (1988). *Psychological testing* (6th ed.). New York: Macmillan.
Banta, T. W. (1987). *Selected bibliography on outcomes assessment*. Knoxville, TN: Assessment Resource Center, University of Tennessee.

Bibliography of assessment instruments. (1987). Knoxville, TN: Assessment Resource Center, University of Tennessee.

Bloom, B. S., et al. (Eds.). (1956). *Taxonomy of educational objectives: The classification of educational goals: Handbook I: Cognitive domain.* New York: David McKay.

Chandler, J. W. (1987). The college perspective on assessment. Proceedings of the 1986 ETS Invitational Conference on Assessing the Outcomes of Higher Education. Princeton, NJ: Educational Testing Service.

College Board and Educational Testing Service. (1986). *Assessment and evaluation instruments for higher education.* Princeton, NJ: Author.

Collier, D. V. (1978). *Program classification structure* (Technical Report No. 106). Boulder, CO: National Center for Higher Education Management Systems at Western Interstate Commission for Higher Education.

Council for the Advancement of Standards for Student Services/Development Programs. (1986). *CAS standards and guidelines for student services/ development programs.* College Park, MD: Office of Student Affairs, University of Maryland.

Council on the Continuing Education Unit. (1984). *Principles of good practice in continuing education.* Silver Spring, MD: Author.

Ewell, P. T. (1983). *Student outcomes questionnaires: An implementation handbook.* Boulder, CO: National Center for Higher Education Management Systems.

Ewell, P. T. (1984). *The self-regulating institution: Information for excellence.* Boulder, CO: National Center for Higher Education Management Systems.

Ewell, P. T. (1985). Levers for change: The role of state government in improving the quality of postsecondary education. [ECS working paper]. Denver, CO: Education Commission of the States.

Ewell, P. T. (1987). Principles of longitudinal enrollment analysis: Conducting retention and student flow studies. In J. Muffo & G. W. McLaughlin (Eds.), *A primer on institutional research.* (pp. 1–19). Tallahassee, FL: Association for Institutional Research.

Fincher, C. (1978). Importance of criteria for institutional goals. In R. H. Fenske (Ed.). *Using goals in research and planning* (pp. 1–15). New Directions for Institutional Research, no. 19. San Francisco: Jossey-Bass.

Fong, B. (1987). The external examiner approach to assessment. Paper commissioned by the American Association for Higher Education Assessment Forum for the Second National Conference on Assessment in Higher Education, Denver, CO.

Forrest, A., & Steele, J. M. (1982). *Defining and measuring general education knowledge and skills.* Technical Report 1976–88. Iowa City, IA: American College Testing Program.

Goldman, B. A., & Osborne, W. L. (1985). *Directory of unpublished experimental mental measures: Volume IV.* New York: Human Sciences Press.

Harris, J. (1985). Assessing outcomes in higher education. In C. Adelman (Ed.), *Assessment in American higher education: Issues and contexts* (pp. 13–31). Washington, DC: U.S. Department of Education.

Henerson, M. E., Morris, L. L., & Fitz-Gibbon, C. T. (1978). *How to measure attitude.* Beverly Hills, CA: Sage.

House, R. M. (1983). *Standards of practice in continuing education: A status study.* Silver Spring, MD: Council on the Continuing Education Unit.

Katchadourian, H. A., & Boli, J. (1985). *Careerism and intellectualism among college students*. San Francisco: Jossey-Bass.

Krathwohl, D. R., Bloom, B. S., & Masia, B. B. (Eds.). (1964). *Taxonomy of educational objectives: The classification of educational goals: Handbook II: Affective domain*. New York: David McKay.

Micek, S. S., Service, A. L., & Lee, Y. S. (1975). *Outcome measures and procedures manual: Field edition* (Technical Report No. 70). Boulder, CO: National Center for Higher Education Management Systems at Western Interstate Commission for Higher Education.

Miller, R. I. (1980). Appraising institutional performance. In P. Jedamus, M. W. Peterson, & Associates (Eds.), *Improving academic management*. San Francisco: Jossey-Bass.

Mitchell, J. V. (Ed.). (1985). *The ninth mental measurements yearbook*. Lincoln, NE: Buros Institute of Mental Measurements.

Mitchell, J. V. (1983). *Tests in print, III*. Lincoln, NE: Buros Institute of Mental Measurements.

Moore, K. M. (1986). Assessment of institutional effectiveness. In J. Losak (Ed.), *Applying institutional research in decision making* (pp. 49–60). New Directions for Community Colleges, no. 56. San Francisco: Jossey-Bass.

Morris, L. L., & Fitz-Gibbon, C. T. (1978). *How to measure achievement*. Beverly Hills, CA: Sage.

Myers, E. M., & Topping, J. R. (1974). *Information exchange procedures activity structure* (Technical Report No. 63). Boulder, CO: National Center for Higher Education Management Systems.

National Laboratory for Higher Education. (1974). *Developing measurable objectives*. Durham, NC: Author.

Pace, C. R. (1983). *College student experiences*. Los Angeles: Higher Education Research Institute, University of California, Los Angeles.

Pascarella, E. T. (1987). Are value-added analyses valuable? Proceedings of the ETS Invitational Conference on Assessing the Outcomes of Higher Education. Princeton, NJ: Educational Testing Service.

Pratt, L. K., & Reichard, D. J. (1983). Assessing institutional goals. In N. P. Uhl (Ed.), *Using research for institutional planning* (pp. 53–66). New Directions for Institutional Research, no. 37. San Francisco: Jossey-Bass.

Resource manual on institutional effectiveness. (1987). Atlanta: Commission on Colleges of the Southern Association of Colleges and Schools.

SAS Users Guide: Basics, Version 5 Edition (1985). Cary, NC: SAS Institute, Inc.

Student Services Program Review Project. (1986). *They said it couldn't be done*. Santa Ana, CA: Author.(ERIC ED 280518)

Study Group on the Conditions of Excellence in American Higher Education. (1984, October 24). Text of new report on excellence in undergraduate education. *Chronicle of Higher Education*, pp. 35–49.

Terenzini, P. T. (1987). The case for unobtrusive measures. Proceedings of the ETS Invitational Conference on Assessing the Outcomes of Higher Education. Princeton, NJ: Educational Testing Service.

Wergin, J. F., & Braskamp, L. A. (Eds.). (1987). *Evaluating administrative services and programs*. New Directions for Institutional Research, no. 56. San Francisco: Jossey-Bass.

CHAPTER FIVE

Initial Implementation

Following 2 years of preparation at the institutional, and subsequently departmental, levels, the institution should be ready for initial operational implementation of institutional effectiveness at the beginning of the third year (shown on Figure 9). By that time the institution should have in place the following key elements developed during the first 2 years of preparation:

1. Expanded Statement of Institutional Purpose—developed during the first year of implementation preparation
2. Statements of Intended Educational, Research, and Service Outcomes as well as Statements of Administrative Objectives— prepared during the second year by each department/program and closely linked to the expanded statement of purpose
3. Assessment Plan—designed in close coordination with departmental/program statements of intentions during the second year

With these three important components serving as the foundation, the institution is ready to begin operational institutional effectiveness implementation; however, a modest amount of institutional remotivation may be necessary to refocus the institution's attention on the task immediately at hand.

At the beginning of the third year, the institution should reflect on what has been accomplished regarding institutional effectiveness, the then current operational implementation activities, and the ultimate value of complete implementation. This process could be accomplished by distribution of a well-prepared document covering these points; however, it probably would best be accomplished through either a single campuswide convocation or through multiple smaller meetings highlighting these points as the document is distributed.

Figure 9

**The Third Year of a Four-Year Plan for
Implementation of Institutional Effectiveness
and Assessment Activities on a Campus**

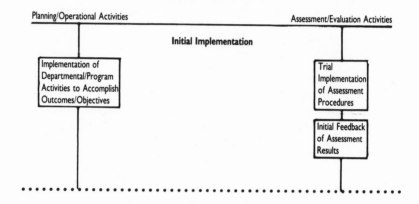

The purpose of this activity, whether written or covered in meetings or both, is to rekindle the enthusiasm and energy with which implementation activities commenced several years earlier and to demonstrate the CEO's continued high level of interest in the subject. Regardless of the success that the first 2 years of preparatory activities have enjoyed, the best and most successful implementation effort will begin to "wilt" after several years of steady work. It is essential that an implementation "pep rally," in one form or another, be held as actual operational implementation begins in order to revitalize those taking part in the implementation process.

As shown on Figure 9, implementation during this third year continues on both the planning/operational and assessment/evaluation tracks. However, the bulk of developmental or new work is focused in "Trial Implementation of Assessment Procedures," while the institution's academic and administrative departments conduct relatively normal operations designed to accomplish their intended outcomes/objectives.

Planning/Operational Activities

Following the considerable amount of departmental/program effort required to establish statements of intended outcomes or objectives during the second year, the degree of involvement by academic and administrative department/program personnel early in the third year of implementation may seem to some like a respite from previous preparatory activities directed toward implementation. In fact, the only activity scheduled on the planning/operational activities track during the third year is "Implementation of Departmental/Program Activities to Accomplish Outcomes/Objectives." Stated differently, academic and administrative departments are not required to do anything except their functional tasks (teaching, research, public service, student registration, maintenance of fiscal records, etc.) and, possibly, assist in the "Trial Implementation of Assessment Procedures" later during the third year of implementation.

Superficially, this appears to be a relatively easy year for the academic and administrative departments/programs within the institution; however, in reality, many departments/programs will be implementing new or substantially revised curricular patterns or services growing from development of their statements of intended outcomes or objectives.

The very act of specifying their intended outcomes or objectives during the second year will lead many departments to consider and then implement improved educational or service activities during the third year. An academic department may have determined that, in order for its degree program graduates to accomplish a particular cognitive outcome, a new course will be required. A research-oriented department may have concluded that to reach its level of intended grant commitment by external agencies, a shift or change in grant application procedures is necessary. In order to accomplish specified objectives regarding student residential life, administrators and staff in student affairs may have determined it necessary to modify greatly the social and educational programs taking place at the institution. In all of these examples the central point is similar: Even as operational implementation of institutional effectiveness is begun and before the implementation of any formal assessment, many of the institution's departments/programs will begin to benefit from their natural response to the challenge of setting intended outcomes or objectives and then seeking to conduct departmental/program operations so as to accomplish those ends.

Within these departmental efforts toward accomplishment of their intended outcomes or objectives, some units may wish to conduct informal or departmental midyear miniassessments of their progress. However, in those units in which substantial changes have taken place in operations, it may well take several years for the full impact of their revised operations to become evident through assessment.

Assessment/Evaluation Activities

Clearly, the bulk of the activity during this initial year of operational implementation of institutional effectiveness will be involved with initiation of assessment procedures and feedback mechanisms.

Both the second year of implementation and the first half of this third year will undoubtedly be filled with the design of and planning for assessment, but it is in the later half of the third year of implementation that Trial Implementation of Assessment Procedures will take place. Assuming that implementation years roughly parallel academic years, trial implementation and feedback would take place during the period between March and August of the third year. This period of time should be evenly divided between assessment activities conducted primarily during the months of March, April, and May and results processing and feedback during June, July, and August.

The assessment-and-feedback cycle should be initiated by the end of the academic year and be completed before the next academic year begins. These timing restraints mean that the majority of the work in this area will take place as faculty and students, who might otherwise be engaged in supporting these activities, are preparing to leave the campus or have actually departed for the summer. Hence, institutions should seriously consider employment of several faculty members (perhaps one from each college or school) and a number of students during the trial implementation summer to assist in processing the data received and preparing the necessary feedback for presentation to the faculty and staff at the beginning of the next academic year. What activities can be expected in the "Trial Implementation of Assessment Procedures"?

The "Trial Implementation of Assessment Procedures" will result in a considerable amount of effort in at least four major areas of endeavor: (a) standardized cognitive testing, (b) administration of attitudinal surveys, (c) information drawn from institutional data bases and other institutional data sources, and (d) departmental reports of assessment means implemented within the department.

Standardized Cognitive Testing

Undoubtedly, the fulfillment of many statements of intended departmental educational outcomes will be assessed through students' performance on standardized cognitive tests. Hence, a substantial increase in the number of students taking such examinations can be anticipated. The procedures implemented for such testing should ensure that students have ample opportunity to take such tests and that students applying for graduation in a particular program register to take the appropriate test. Three basic questions will emerge concerning increased student participation in cognitive testing:

1. Who pays for such standardized examinations?
2. Should achievement of a specific score be required for graduation?
3. How can the institution motivate students to take such examinations seriously if a "passing" score is not required for graduation?

The answer to the first two of these logical inquiries relates to the primary purpose for the administration of the standardized examinations—assessment of institutional effectiveness. Although performance on such examinations will reflect on individual students, the primary intent is to assess the effectiveness of the institution's educational programs, not its students. Hence, either asking students to pay directly for taking standardized tests or setting a passing score for students to attain before graduation appears to be inconsistent with the primary purpose of administration. However, this statement should not be construed as opposition to increasing the general student activity fee or tuition sufficiently to cover assessment-related costs.

Assuming that students are not required to pay directly for taking such standardized tests or to achieve a "passing" score, how are institutions going to get students to take such standardized examinations seriously? The answer is that each institution must seek and encourage voluntary compliance by specifically explaining to students why their taking the examination is important to continued institutional improvement. Institutions may further seek voluntary compliance by describing to students the potential benefit of having such standardized examination results on file when they graduate. However, the undeniable fact remains that, short of requiring a passing score, institutions cannot force students to take standardized examinations. Given this realization, institutions should limit the pressure placed upon students to take such standardized examinations and be prepared to disregard test scores that appear to reflect halfhearted participation.

Attitudinal Surveys

Also taking place during this period of time will be distribution to and return of attitudinal surveys by those students completing educational programs at the institution. These instruments, designed and pilot tested earlier in the implementation process, are best distributed and collected during the student's administrative processing for graduation. Some institutions may find it useful to distribute the survey at the time students obtain their application for graduation and to collect the completed questionnaire at the time a diploma fee is paid.

Other attitudinal surveys such as those of alumni, students leaving the institution prior to graduation, or employers are less constrained within the March-to-August time frame. In order to spread the workload of the trial assessment procedures implementation over the entire year, institutions should consider distribution of attitudinal surveys to such recipients during the period prior to March to avoid scheduling this activity concurrently with other assessment procedures more directly tied to the last half of the year.

Information Drawn from Institutional Data Systems

As the academic year draws to a close, data concerning student achievements, retention, and other subjects should be drawn from the institution's data system (as well as the data systems of other institutions) to support the assessment process. Data drawn from other institutions' data systems will be necessary to ascertain the success of students transferring from two-year colleges to four-year institutions and later to gauge the success in graduate school of baccalaureate program graduates.

Departmental Reports

During May and June, the institution's academic departments can be expected to be administering various cognitive and performance measures which they have designed both for assessment of the extent to which their intended programmatic outcomes have been achieved and, potentially, as requirements for student graduation. Although such means of assessment must be administered at the departmental level, there must also be institutional responsibility and effort to ensure that such activities are actually undertaken by the responsible departments and that the results are forwarded to a central point for compilation with other assessment results relating to the program.

Assembly and Processing of Assessment Results

During the early to mid-summer of the third year of implementation, the institution should be literally awash in assessment-related data. Student scores for standardized cognitive tests taken earlier should be arriving. The results of attitudinal surveys (particularly the graduates' survey) will become available. Data drawn from institutional sources and other databases should have been processed. Departmental assessment measure results should be available. How should this flood of data be organized and refined into useful assessment information for the departments/programs and the institution?

The key to organizing this variety of assessment data is the establishment of a centralized agency (office, department, etc.) to which all such data are forwarded for compilation. Within that agency (staffed by both its own permanent employees and temporary faculty and students), separate folders or files for each department/program establishing intended departmental outcomes or objectives should be established. The folder should contain a copy of the departmental statements of intention (including their proposed means for assessment) and all of the trial assessment implementation results relating to that department/program. During the early part of the summer, it will be necessary that an outcome-by-outcome (or objective-by-objective) comparison of the proposed means of assessment with the results in the folder be conducted. The comparison and subsequent follow-up will determine which data are missing from the folder but available within the institution and which intended means of assessment were, for one reason or another, not accomplished. By the end of June all assessment data available should have been collected and filed in the appropriate folder by department/program prior to analysis and preparation of feedback to the departments.

Initial Feedback of Results

Once the results of the trial assessment procedure implementation are received and filed, analysis of the results and preparation of feedback should commence. Analysis of such results will always remain a matter of subjective judgment at the departmental/program level, and only limited centralized analysis of results need, or indeed should, be provided to the department. On the other hand, centralized organization of the information to focus upon departmental statements of intentions, summarization of individual student results into departmental/program averages, or interpretation of departmental/program results in light of institutional or national normative data may greatly enhance a department's willingness and ability to analyze and apply the results of the trial assessment procedures.

Although little direct analysis of results needs to be provided to the departmental/program level, a general need exists at the institutional level for insight into the extent to which the institution is accomplishing its Expanded Statement of Institutional Purpose. If the statement of purpose portrays the institution as a selective entity whose graduates should excel academically, but the trial assessment results indicate that its students are consistently exhibiting cognitive learning levels that might be expected of graduates at a substantially less selective institution, the institution should seriously consider adjusting its Expanded Statement of Institutional Purpose. Those individuals responsible at the institutional level for analysis and departmental/ program information preparation will undoubtedly form general opinions concerning the extent to which departmental/program statements of intentions are being realized. Through these generalizations (subject to confirmation by individual departmental personnel) a basic understanding of the extent to which intentions expressed in the Expanded Statement of Institutional Purpose are being accomplished can be established.

The means for and timing of the feedback of assessment results to the departmental/program level are crucial to their use for improvement of the institution. During design of the assessment process, considerable thought should have been given to the data processing needed to obtain the desired data layouts and tables regarding each means of assessment. Following assembly of the various assessment results relating to each department/program by each intended outcome/objective, a relatively standardized set of data presentation formats—designed earlier—for the results of each assessment means (cognitive test, attitudinal survey, etc.) should be completed.

There is no intention to homogenize departmental/program data analysis or presentation by use of standardized information formats. Rather, the intention is to devote considerable time and expertise to design of a professionally developed set of data formats which can be quickly and efficiently adapted to each outcome/objective and assessment means. The use of such formats also precludes the expenditure of an inordinate amount of time summarizing the data for each outcome/objective by an individual (faculty or student) very possibly not trained in data analysis or presentation techniques.

To the maximum extent feasible, feedback of the assessment results should be part of a face-to-face report presented by a representative of the assessment team to the department/program. Such a presentation not only explains the results more clearly and provides an opportunity for the answering of questions but also enhances the professional and collegial image of the assessment team and stimulates greater use of the results within the department/program. The use of faculty employed during the summer to support the assessment effort in feedback seminars in their college/school should be given serious consideration.

Without much doubt, the most appropriate time to present assessment feedback results is as the institution begins its next academic year. At that time all of the faculty will be present, and the tradition of starting anew will facilitate review of past accomplishments, revision of statements of departmental/program intentions, or adjustment of operational activities to better accomplish current intentions.

Unfortunately, taking advantage of the beginning of the academic year as the period for assessment feedback across the institution means that a great deal of information must be conveyed in a short period. For this task to be accomplished, sets of feedback presentation data must be prepared before the beginning of the academic year, and for several weeks those involved with presenting departmental/program assessment seminars must conduct several such seminars each day. Regardless of the effort involved, there is no more crucial portion of the assessment process than successful feedback of the results.

Expectations for Initial Implementation

What is reasonable to expect from the institution's initial operational implementation of institutional effectiveness in this third year? Anything less than chaos should be considered a substantial success. It must be borne in mind that what should be taking place is perhaps the most pervasive and comprehensive change in the institution's means of doing business in many years and that this initial implementation is simply going to be a bit bumpy.

On many campuses incomplete implementation may be the rule

rather than the exception. However, during this initial implementation evidence of a good-faith effort to implement the assessment plan is as important, if not more so, than the comprehensiveness or precision of this initial implementation, which should be viewed as a pilot test of the assessment and feedback procedures designed.

As the third year of implementation of institutional effectiveness (and the first year of operational implementation) draws to a close, the institution should accentuate the positive through press releases concerning the most successful aspects of the "Trial Assessment Procedures Implementation." It should also emphasize concrete examples of the benefits that the campus and students can expect to gain through "Initiation of the Annual Institutional Assessment Cycle" during the fourth year of implementation. In addition, the institution should treat generously those who have contributed most to successful implementation as an incentive to others to act in a similar manner as the annual cycle is implemented in the following year.

CHAPTER SIX

Establishment of the Annual Institutional Effectiveness Cycle

The work of the three previous years will have resulted in substantive planning/operational and assessment/evaluation accomplishments. Among the planning/operational accomplishments will be "Establishment of an Expanded Statement of Institutional Purpose"; "Identification of Intended Educational, Research, and Public Service Outcomes"; "Establishment of Administrative Objectives"; and "Implementation of Departmental/Program Activities to Accomplish Outcomes/Objectives Identified" (see Figure 3, p. 20). Assessment/evaluation activities during the first three years can best be summarized as the design and initial implementation of a comprehensive program of evaluation and assessment of the extent to which institutional intentions—expressed in the expanded statement of purpose—are being fulfilled through departmental/program actions.

Just as the third year has drawn to a close, feedback from the initial implementation of assessment/evaluation activities will be forwarded to the institutional level as well as to the department/program level. The receipt and consideration of this information initiate the series of events that will be repeated each year and that become the basis for practical implementation of the Institutional Effectiveness Paradigm shown in Figure 3 and further illustrated in Figure 10 as the **Annual Institutional Effectiveness Cycle (AIEC)**.

The establishment of the Annual Institutional Effectiveness Cycle is of paramount importance on the campus. Institutions tend to operate on an annual cycle of events conditioned by the academic year and

Figure 10

**Final Year of a Four-Year Plan for
Implementation of Institutional Effectiveness
and Assessment Activities on a Campus**

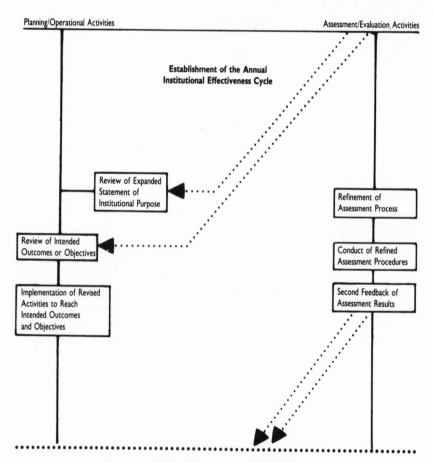

REPEAT FOURTH-YEAR ACTIVITIES—CONDUCT COMPREHENSIVE
INSTITUTIONAL AND PROCESS EVALUATION IN EIGHTH YEAR

the annual budgetary process. If implementation of institutional effectiveness is to become part of the institution's normal or routine method of doing business, then it must become a part of the yearly sequence of events expected at the institution.

Initiation of the Annual Institutional Effectiveness Cycle must be based upon the accomplisments (planning/operational and assessment/evaluation) made during the first 3 years of implementation. The AIEC turns what probably had been on some campuses episodic and discontinuous efforts toward assessment for instructional improvement into an ongoing program of institutional improvement. It is simply unreasonable to expect that an institution can divert sufficient resources (time of current employees and additional out-of-pocket expenditures) in a single year to accomplish effectively all of the necessary tasks among the planning/operational and assessment/evaluation activities described earlier. Even if sufficient resources were provided, the campuswide political ramifications of such an effort could easily preclude its success. In order to consider institutional effectiveness annually and to integrate it into the routine of campus operations, these accomplishments must be firmly established so that they can be *reviewed, adjusted,* and *evaluated* as part of the Annual Institutional Effectiveness Cycle.

On many campuses excellent programs of instructional assessment and evaluation have flourished. Unfortunately, very few of these programs have been comprehensive or long-lived. There are many explanations for the limited scope and relatively short life of many of these programs. Too often the most common explanations relate to the establishment of such programs in response to the interests of an individual, who may subsequently change positions, or the requirements of a professional or regional accreditating body, whose periodic program reviews, once completed, often are quickly forgotten. Establishment of the Annual Institutional Effectiveness Cycle replaces transient personnel and external motivation with the systematic review, adjustment, and evaluation of institutional operations as part of the ongoing institutional process.

As the institution approaches implementation of the Annual Institutional Effectiveness Cycle in the fourth year of implementation activities, a certain amount of remotivation must take place. Although the institution's reward systems should have demonstrated not only the need for but also the wisdom in departmental program implementation during the first 3 years, a summary type of document regarding current status (accomplishments during the past 3 years) and components of the Annual Institutional Effectiveness Cycle to be undertaken in each of the coming years should be prepared and widely distributed. The role of the CEO in solid support of institutional effectiveness implementation should be visible to all as he or she leads the review of the Expanded Statement of Institutional Purpose, directs resource allocation in support of institutional goals, and administers his or her office's objectives. The components of the Annual Institutional Effectiveness Cycle are as shown in Figure 10 and described in the following paragraphs.

Planning/Operational Activities in the Annual Institutional Effectiveness Cycle

The primary planning/operational activities conducted each year as part of the Annual Institutional Effectiveness Cycle relate to the review and, if needed, revision of institutional and departmental statements of intentions. At both levels, these actions are initiated at the earliest part of the annual cycle (July through August) by receipt of assessment results from the previous year's cycle.

At the institutional level, activity is centered around review and revision of the Expanded Statement of Institutional Purpose. Based upon analysis of the results of the previous year's assessment (as generalized and focused at the institutional level), a decision should be reached annually regarding the general feasibility of the current Expanded Statement of Institutional Purpose and its goals statements in particular. Should analysis of the assessment results emanating from the previous year indicate substantially less accomplishment than intended, then a value judgment must be made concerning either adjustment downward of institutional expectations or renewal of efforts to accomplish potentially unrealistic institutional aspirations. Although the decision to renew efforts may be more politically palatable and defensible over the short run, the institution's intentions eventually should be aligned with its accomplishments as revealed through assessment results reported annually.

Review of the Expanded Statement of Institutional Purpose should be conducted relatively quickly and with input from external data sources. Each year, the review should be conducted within the first several weeks of the AIEC by a relatively small representative group headed by the institution's CEO. There is no reason to replicate the effort that went into establishing the Expanded Statement of Institutional Purpose. Rather, the focus should be upon review and adjustment of the statement based upon assessment results and, at those institutions practicing strategic planning, information concerning environmental fit, or the relationship of the institution to its external environment.

The result of review and adjustment of the Expanded Statement of Institutional Purpose will be the establishment of such a statement validated for the then current Annual Institutional Effectiveness Cycle. This statement should be distributed widely on the campus within the first several weeks of the cycle as the basis for further activities.

At the departmental/program level, the Annual Institutional Effectiveness Cycle is initiated based upon receipt of the previous year's assessment results and the current cycle's Expanded Statement of Institutional Purpose. Each department/program is initially called upon to compare the results of the previous year's assessment with the intended outcomes or objectives for that period. Undoubtedly, assessment results will reveal outcomes or objectives that are being overrealized as well as ones that are not being completely achieved or for which the results are inconclusive.

In the case of overrealization, departments/programs will probably adjust their statements of intended outcomes or objectives upward to match their accomplishments. In the case of those intended outcomes or objectives whose assessment indicates that they are not being met, departments/programs should determine whether to lower their expectations or revise their procedures or activities designed to accomplish their intentions. It is vitally important—particularly in the institution's academic departments—that consideration of the previous year's assessment results and the adjustment of departmental statements of intentions (as just described) be undertaken by the department/program as a whole, with emphasis upon input from all faculty or staff involved and their ultimate identification with the decision reached.

An important part of this departmental/program consideration of the previous year's assessment results is the evaluation of those results themselves. Particularly in those cases in which assessment results appear incomplete or contradictory regarding an intended outcome or objective, departments should review carefully the adequacy, validity, and completeness of the assessment results provided. The results of this review should be reported to those individuals responsible for conducting the institution's assessment/evaluation activities so that the problems identified can be corrected in the following AIEC.

In addition to reviewing the results of assessment related to its departmental/program intentions, each unit should carefully review the then current Expanded Statement of Institutional Purpose and compare it with the previous year's purpose statement. Such a review may provide the basis and impetus for revision of departmental/program statements of intentions, which must remain linked to the current institutional statement of intentions.

The results of departmental/program review and any revisions will be a current set of intended outcomes or objectives for this Annual Institutional Effectiveness Cycle. This set of departmental/program statements should be finalized by the beginning of the fall semester each year. As future iterations of the AIEC take place, progressively fewer adjustments to such statements should be expected.

The balance of the planning/operational activities (roughly September through July) will focus upon departmental/program activities designed to accomplish the refined departmental/program statements of intended outcomes or objectives. Departments should bear in mind that it may take several iterations of the Annual Institutional Effectiveness Cycle for changes in departmental policies, actions, curricula, and so forth to be reflected fully in assessment results.

In summary, planning/operational activities during the Annual Institutional Effectiveness Cycle are loaded into the first several months of each cycle with review of assessment results and revision, if needed, of institutional and departmental/program statements of intention. The balance of the year is devoted to normal institutional and departmental operations aimed toward accomplishment of the statements of purpose and of intended outcomes/objectives.

Assessment/Evaluation Activities in the Annual Institutional Effectiveness Cycle

Each year the assessment/evaluation activities associated with the Annual Institutional Effectiveness Cycle will be comprised of three actions: (a) review of the previous year's assessment activities and "Refinement of Assessment Process," (b) "Conduct of Refined Assessment Procedures," and (c) the "Feedback of Assessment Results" to the departmental/program and institutional levels as the basis for the next year's cycle (see Figure 10).

Although the bulk of actual assessment/evaluation work each year will take place in the last 4 to 5 months of the annual cycle, a critical review of the previous year's assessment/evaluation activities and refinement of such procedures should take place within the first several months of each year's cycle. Information concerning the previous year's assessment/evaluation activities will come from the departments/programs being serviced and from those individuals coordinating the assessment/evaluation program. As part of the feedback mechanism, departments/programs should be submitting reports concerning both gaps in assessment/evaluation coverage of their statements of intentions and seemingly contradictory results that require further technical review. Additionally, those charged with coordinating and conducting the assessment/evaluation activities will, doubtlessly, have a list of problems encountered during the previous year which they do not wish to repeat. Typically, this problem list will be fairly extensive in the initial AIEC iterations but will be shortened with successive refinements of the procedures.

In addition to a review of recent assessment/evaluation efforts, assessment procedures will need to be updated in light of both campus and external changes. On campus, those charged with coordination of assessment/evaluation activities will need to ensure that changes to departmental/program statements of intentions are incorporated into the assessment plan and that adequate coverage is provided. Additionally, changes in and additions to assessment/evaluation technology (standardized testing instruments, licensure examinations, survey instruments and techniques, etc.) should be considered for incorporation into the institution's refined assessment/evaluation procedures.

The results of the review and updating of institutional assessment/evaluation procedures should be a refined assessment/evaluation plan for implementation during the second half of the Annual Institutional Effectiveness Cycle. During early iterations of the cycle, implementation of the assessment/evaluation plan can be expected to focus upon smoothing implementation mechanics, filling gaps in coverage of assessment/evaluation procedures, and increasing the efficiency of the process.

With any operation as large and complex as the process of implementing assessment/evaluation activities on a campus there are bound to be a substantial number of "bumps," "stumbles," and apparent failures in initial implementation. There will be simply too many unforeseen and uncontrollable variables for which to plan initially. Once the process has been implemented on a trial basis, these problems will surface and will take several iterations to reduce to a manageable level—although a comprehensive institutional assessment/evaluation inevitably involves a degree of discomfort.

Likewise, initial implementation of the assessment/evaluation plan can be expected to leave considerable gaps in coverage of departmental/program intentions. These gaps will exist for numerous reasons, and over the years most will be filled by one or more assessment/ evaluation techniques.

Once active implementation begins, one of the greatest possible improvements in assessment/evaluation techniques may occur: increased efficiency in conducting the process. A considerable portion of the initial year's implementation time will result from the inherent inefficiency in starting most processes. As the years progress, expenditures for assessment/evaluation should remain relatively constant; however, efficiency gained in implementation should be expected to offset (partially or completely) cost escalations and expansion of the process to fill gaps. The final assessment/evaluation activity conducted each year as a portion of the Annual Institutional Effectiveness Cycle is the provision of assessment/evaluation results—otherwise known as feedback—which acts as the stimulus for the next year's cycle. Although this activity will transpire in the last several weeks of the cycle, review of reactions by the departments/programs to the feedback techniques used in the previous year should be gathered early in the cycle with departmental/program reactions to the assessment/evaluation results.

Two important improvements in early feedback procedures should be possible in succeeding years. First, by accumulation of results over several years, the limited number, or N, of results concerning certain programs should be mitigated and greater confidence established in the combined results of several years. Second, refinements in techniques should lead to increased utilization of graphic and narrative forms of feedback and the gradual deemphasizing of tabular data presentation.

Summary

Shown as Figure 11 is a month-by-month representation of the Annual Institutional Effectiveness Cycle which might be typical of those institutions operating on an "early semester" calendar and a June 30 to July 1 fiscal year. This timing would necessarily need to be modified at those institutions with significantly different academic and fiscal cycles.

Figure 11
Annual Institutional Effectiveness
Cycle Applied to an Academic
Year Sequence (Early Semester)

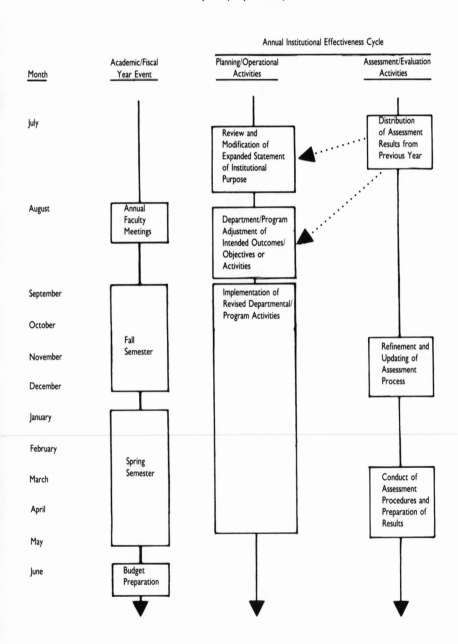

The establishment of the Annual Institutional Effectiveness Cycle and the continuing program of institutional study/assessment/ evaluation which it represents is the final process-oriented result of the implementation process. However, the final actual result is an institution taking purposeful actions toward its intended ends, assessing/evaluating its results to date, and adjusting its future actions to be more successful.

CHAPTER SEVEN

Maintaining Institutional Effectiveness Operations Over an Extended Period of Time

The initial work to implement institutional effectiveness on a campus may have appeared to be an almost insurmountable hurdle, but the maintenance of institutional effectiveness operations over an extended period of time represents an even greater challenge. Assuming that an institution has put into place the Annual Institutional Effectiveness Cycle described in the previous chapter and that it wishes to continue such operations, there are further developmental phases that can be expected and forces that will affect successful continuation.

During the fourth through approximately the seventh years of implementation, the campus should report on the Annual Institutional Effectiveness Cycle. In addition to the smoothing-out process inherent in the cycle, several other adjustments should take place during this period.

First, and most important, each year minor adjustments should be made in the Expanded Statement of Institutional Purpose in reaction to the generalized assessment findings of the previous cycle and changes in the institution's external environment. Additionally, relatively substantial changes should take place in departmental/program statements of intentions during the first several years of cycle implementation as a result of the detailed assessment/evaluation results provided. If either institutional or departmental/program statements of intention remain static from year to year, institutional effectiveness is not being taken seriously and will ultimately be discontinued at the institution as a pointless exercise.

During the fourth through the seventh years of implementation, a task almost as important as institutional adjustments of statements of intentions is the gradual expansion of the assessment plan to address service gaps in initial coverage and utilize assessment/evaluation methods developed to date. Without doubt, gaps in coverage and inconsistent results will emerge from the assessment/evaluation activities undertaken during the first several years of implementation of the Annual Institutional Effectiveness Cycle. As problems are resolved, major adjustments in and expansion of assessment/evaluation activities as well as implementation of newly developed means of assessment should occur each year.

Finally, during the period of Annual Institutional Effectiveness Cycle implementation in years 4 through 7 of implementation, substantive improvement can be expected in feedback procedures and in the extent to which departments/programs understand the results. Part of this improvement in communication and understanding of the results can be attributed to both increasing familiarity with the assessment/evaluation results provided to departments/programs each year and the improvement in feedback mechanisms utilized each year.

Comprehensive Review of Institutional Effectiveness Operations

The basic philosophy behind institutional effectiveness is that of stating an institution's intentions, conducting activities, and assessing/ evaluating the extent to which the institution's intentions have been accomplished. This same philosophy must also guide institutional effectiveness operations themselves. In approximately the eighth year of implementation (after four complete repetitions of the AIEC) a thorough assessment of institutional effectiveness operations should take place.

Such a comprehensive assessment should probably have both procedural and substantive components. Each of the components (activities) during the Annual Institutional Effectiveness Cycle should be reviewed regarding its internal merits and the manner in which that element is functioning as a portion of the annual cycle. From the substantive perspective, the institution should conduct a thorough review and updating of its Expanded Statement of Institutional Purpose as well as its departmental/programmatic statements of intended outcomes/administrative objectives. Although adjustments and refinements to these statements should be expected annually, these actions cannot take the place of a periodically conducted thoughtful and extended reconsideration of the institution's and departments'/programs' basic purposes or intentions.

The comprehensive review of institutional effectiveness operations envisioned should take the better portion of a year. Hence, it is suggested that the Annual Institutional Effectiveness Cycle be discontinued during the year in which the comprehensive review takes place and resumed the following year, using the changes suggested from the review.

Forces Impeding Continuation of Institutional Effectiveness Operations

A number of natural and understandable forces that impede long-term continuation of institutional effectiveness operations on a campus can be expected to come into play. These same forces tend to thwart long-term continuation of all except absolutely essential (registration, budgeting, etc.) activities.

The first of these forces is what can be characterized as institutional exhaustion or loss of interest. Frankly, institutional effectiveness operations are not absolutely essential to maintaining an institution (registering students, holding classes, conducting research, etc.)—only to leading an institution toward accomplishment of its stated intentions. After the period of additional effort required to implement the Annual Institutional Effectiveness Cycle, many individuals will tend to consider the matter accomplished and want to return to maintaining the institution in the manner in which it had been functioning earlier.

Naturally complementing this tendency toward regression to previous methods of operations may well be the departure from the institution of those individuals most responsible for institutional effectiveness implementation. Normal personnel turbulence during the period of time between initial implementation and comprehensive review of the process will result in the loss of a number of personnel instrumental in institutional effectiveness implementation and personally identified with such operations. There is also some likelihood that a disproportionately heavy share of turnover among faculty and key staff will be among those most responsible for institutional effectiveness implementation as their progressive ideas and actions are recognized and they are selected for positions of greater responsibility. Such action may leave those less supportive of institutional effectiveness to greet the replacements. It should be observed that these replacements will probably not be personally identified with institutional effectiveness to the extent that their predecessors were and that these replacements may well be less enthusiastic about continuation of institutional effectiveness operations as they seek to make their own mark on the institution.

Both institutional exhaustion and personnel turnover can be described as passive impediments to continued institutional effectiveness operations; some members of the campus community, however, may actively resist continuation. This active resistance is likely to arise from individuals who are philosophically opposed to institutional effectiveness or whose personal interests are not best met by the process. Even following successful implementation of the Annual Institutional Effectiveness Cycle, some members of the campus community will remain unalterably opposed philosopically to institutional effectiveness because they do not believe the results of the educational process are assessable. On the other (more pragmatic) hand, some individuals will continue to see their own personal ends as better served through a less objective (and frequently more political) decision-making process. These people will oppose continuation on grounds more publicly acceptable than vested self-interest, but with a single aim in mind. Active opposition to continuation of institutional effectiveness operations can be expected to increase from both of these groups as the proponents of institutional effectiveness depart, their less committed replacements arrive, and institutional commitment becomes less apparent.

Marshalling Forces to Encourage Continuation of Institutional Effectiveness Operations

Without the long-term existence on a campus of a "true believer" in institutional effectiveness or a senior member of the administrative staff closely identified with the concept, there is an excellent chance that institutional effectiveness operations will gradually diminish. There must be an individual to champion the cause of continuation, and that person must have the active and visible support of the CEO. If such a person exists and is supported by the CEO, he or she can call into play a number of forces that will facilitate continuation of institutional effectiveness operations.

From a philosophical standpoint, proponents of institutional effectiveness can argue the intrinsic value of the process and support this assertion with examples of institutional and departmental/program improvements that have been brought about through institutional effectiveness. This is potentially one of the strongest inducements toward continued support by a substantial segment of the campus community, but this argument will have little impact on those actively opposed to continuation.

Another strong motivation toward continued implementation of institutional effectiveness operations may be external pressure in the form of regional and professional accreditation requirements. With implementation of the current national movement toward increased emphasis on assessment of student learning outcomes as part of accreditation requirements, institutions will be required to document their activities in institutional effectiveness and outcomes assessment by an increasing number of accrediting bodies. Such activities are obviously not easily initiated in a short period of time, and institutions desiring to have their various professional and specific regional accreditations reaffirmed will find it far easier to continue their existing institutional effectiveness operations than to reinitiate such operations in response to the demands of various external accrediting bodies.

For public institutions external pressure from accrediting agencies may not be the only form of pressure being exerted from beyond the campus. As stated earlier, a number of central governing boards and state legislatures are currently requiring information regarding institutional practices concerning outcomes assessment or institutional effectiveness. Thus, pressure from the agencies that provide funding to public institutions can be a significant factor in the continuation of institutional effectiveness operations.

Both the intrinsic value of institutional effectiveness and potential external pressure should serve to foster continuation of institutional effectiveness operations, but the best motivation to that end is the incorporation of these operations into the recurring annual series of events at the institution. Just as naturally as fall semester registration is expected to take place in the last week of August, review of the Expanded Statement of Institutional Purpose and departmental/program statements of intentions should be anticipated during the first 3 weeks in August. Just as operational budgets are expected to become effective July 1 each year, assessment findings or results should arrive in the institution's departments during the last week in July. Before students take part in graduation exercises each spring, they are expected to have completed cognitive or performance testing in their major and to have returned their graduating student questionnaire. Institutional effectiveness operations should become the norm or expectation, and breaking that momentum should become just as difficult as was breaking the inertia of institutional resistance when such operations were initiated.

Despite significant forces operating to impede long-term continuation of institutional effectiveness operations, sufficient incentives, motivation, and means exist to support successful long-term institutional effectiveness practices for the welfare of the institution and those whom it would serve.

Our University
Expanded Statement of
Institutional Purpose

OUR UNIVERSITY STATEMENT
OF INSTITUTIONAL MISSION

Our University is an independent, nonsectarian, coeducational institution in the tradition of the liberal arts and sciences. Seeking to be faithful to the ideals of its heritage, Our University is committed, in all of its policies and practices, to the unrestricted and rigorous pursuit of truth, to the centrality of values in human life, and to a respect for differing points of view.

Our mission is to provide an outstanding education for a relatively small number of talented and highly motivated students from a diversity of geographic, ethnic, and socioeconomic backgrounds. To achieve this end, we recruit and retain outstanding faculty members who are dedicated to the art of teaching and advising; to the search for and dissemination of truth through scholarship, research, and creative endeavor; and to service to the university and the larger community. We also seek to provide a supportive and challenging environment in which students can realize the full potential of their abilities and come to understand their responsibility of service in the human community.

The principal focus of Our University's curricular programs is undergraduate education in the liberal arts and sciences, combined with a number of directly career related and preprofessional fields. Relations between the liberal arts and the career-related and preprofessional fields are carefully nurtured to provide mutually reinforcing intellectual experiences for students and faculty. Our University also offers master's and doctoral degree programs in selected professional areas that will prepare individuals for positions of leadership in their chosen careers. In addition, recognizing its responsibility to the larger community, Our University provides a variety of carefully selected programs of continuing education and cultural enrichment. Finally, Our University recognizes its responsibility in maintaining a position of excellence and leadership in research.

In its recruitment and retention of members of the university community, Our University, consistent with its academic and institutional heritage, maintains an openness to all qualified persons.

OUR UNIVERSITY STATEMENT OF INSTITUTIONAL GOALS

I. INTRODUCTION

The "Statement of Institutional Mission" just presented expresses a vision of what our institution intends to be and do. The purpose of the present document is to set forth specific goals for each major area of the university for the next five years, with the conviction that the achievement of these goals will lead to the fulfillment of Our University's stated mission.

It must be recognized that such achievement is contingent upon a number of circumstances, including the availability of adequate financial and other resources. Indeed, decisions regarding essentially academic matters must sometimes be based, at least in part, upon factors that are themselves not specifically academic in nature. What immediately follows in this introduction, therefore, is a summary of certain economic assumptions (i.e., matters over which the university has little or no control), planning parameters, and implications that are presupposed in the following sections of the document.

A. *Economic Assumptions*
   1. Inflation will remain at approximately 4 to 5% over the next 5 years.
   2. Financial support to private institutions and students by state and federal agencies will tend to be reduced in the next 5 years.
   3. The annual income from the current unrestricted endowment sources will remain relatively fixed over the next 5 years.

B. *Planning Parameters*
   1. The student–faculty ratio (FTE students to FTE faculty) will stabilize at 13 to 1 by 1992–93.
   2. The Education and General (E & G) Budget (the basic operating budget) will increase between 7% and 8% each year in the next 5 years and will reach approximately $50 million in the 1992–93 academic year.

3. Annual giving will increase moderately between now and 1993.
4. Adequate fiscal reserves should be created or enlarged to allow for the timely renovation of campus buildings and other facilities.
5. Annual tuition rate increases will be approximately 7% in each of the next 5 years.

C. *Implications*

1. By the 1992–93 academic year, the total number of under-graduate students will stabilize at approximately 4,000.
2. The number of entering freshmen will increase by approximately 30 per year and will reach a class size of approximately 1,200 by the 1992–93 academic year.
3. Efforts will be made to increase the number of applications for admission each year so that we obtain 3,200 applications from highly qualified students by 1992–93.
4. The proportion of the undergraduate students who attend on a full-time basis will increase by approximately 1% per year for the next 5 years.
5. The attrition rate will be reduced by .5% per year for each of the next 5 years.
6. The increasing number of undergraduate students will create the need for a new residence hall in the 1991–92 academic year.
7. To accommodate more undergraduate students, funds should be dedicated to development of more playing/athletic fields.
8. To accommodate the needs of our changing student body, we will need to renovate/add to the University Center.

II. ACADEMIC AFFAIRS

The goal of Our University is to be one of the leading independent liberal arts and sciences universities in the nation, as measured by the quality of its faculty, the strength of its curriculum and academic programs, the effectiveness of its support services, and the excellence of its graduates. Significant steps already have been taken toward achievement of this goal through continued offering of both liberal arts programs designed to impart a depth of understanding in the major field and preprofessional programs preparing the graduate for employment upon graduation. Although the following goals do not represent the totality of intellectual and administrative activity within academic affairs, they do represent focal points for action in the near future.

A. *Curriculum and Academic Programs*

Our University is committed to offering all students a distinctive and challenging academic foundation in liberal studies in order to enhance their communication and analytic skills; to provide an understanding of their intellectual and cultural heritage; and to assist them in the development of self-awareness, responsible leadership, and the capacity to make reasoned moral judgments. Our University will continue to offer the range of disciplines basic to a liberal education and will maintain a balance in the undergraduate curriculum among the humanities, fine arts, behavioral sciences, natural sciences, and selected preprofessional programs. The following goals are of high priority:

1. Study the university's general education program to determine whether revisions are desirable.
2. Initiate more varied forms of instruction for entering students, such as freshman seminars.
3. Establish a process to identify systematically those academic programs that should be targeted for qualitative enhancement and/or numerical growth. The principal criteria to be employed in making these judgments should be centrality to our mission, quality of the existing program, demand, cost-effectiveness, and comparative advantage in offering the program.
4. Encourage new academic program initiatives, particularly of an interdisciplinary nature, that reflect emerging intellectual perspectives and are appropriate to the mission of Our University.
5. Encourage the development of new minors and areas of concentration that complement existing degree programs and are responsive to student interests and societal needs.
6. Be responsive to the continuing education needs of local businesses and industries in areas in which Our University is academically strong.

B. *Graduate and Research Programs*

Although the primary academic thrust of Our University will continue to be its undergraduate program of instruction, graduate education and research will play an increasing role in support of the institution and its attraction and retention of outstanding students and faculty. Within this secondary academic role, Our University will seek during the next 5 years to

1. Develop a limited number of additional graduate-level programs in areas in which the institution maintains a strong undergraduate program, sufficient student demand is evidenced, and local or regional demand for graduates is identified.
2. Review current graduate programs to determine the academic and economic feasibility of their continuation.
3. Increase the level of organized or sponsored research expenditures by 5% per year for the next 5 years.
4. Focus the development of proposals for externally funded or organized research on subjects directly related to local/regional industries or those subjects of particular interest to foundations with which Our University has enjoyed a continuing relationship.

C. *Continuing Education/Public Service*

While maintaining primary commitments to teaching and research, Our University is also committed to helping to meet the continuing education and cultural enrichment needs of our surrounding community. In the next 5 years Our University's goals are to

1. Offer noncredit instruction targeted to meet the continuing education needs of Our University's faculty, staff, and surrounding community. Such programs should not duplicate the efforts of two- and four-year postsecondary institutions within a 25-mile radius of Our University.
2. Provide cultural enrichment opportunities for the university and surrounding community through an artist/lecture/concert series.
3. Offer in-service specialized short courses and seminars for local business and industry.

D. *Faculty*

Persons who combine a love of teaching with a continuing curiosity and a passion for learning, scholarship, research, and creativity are the most important resources of the university. Excellent teaching and advising are essential to the fulfillment of the mission of Our University, as is the conduct of both basic and applied research that contributes to the advancement of knowledge and to the consideration of important societal problems. Various steps have already been taken to develop and maintain an excellent faculty, and the following goals are particularly important:

1. Maintain salaries at highly competitive levels in order to attract a diverse faculty noted for its teaching excellence, scholarly achievements, and dedication to the highest standards of professional activity.
2. Continue to emphasize research and scholarly activity through research assistants' support, travel funds, library materials, adequate access to computer facilities, and other forms of faculty development such as academic leaves and summer stipends.
3. Continue to develop the emphasis placed on advising and working directly with individual students.

E. *Students*

Our University will remain an institution of modest size with a total enrollment of no more than 4,000 students. In the recruitment of all students emphasis is placed on potential for the very highest in academic achievement; leadership, special talents and abilities; and diversity in geographic origin, ethnicity, and socioeconomic status. Appropriate scholarships and need-based financial aid programs will be administered to facilitate recruitment and retention of these students, continuing the significant advances made in the early 1980s.

1. Our University seeks to make it possible for each student to experience the academic and cultural diversity of the university, and the following academic goals for the composition of the student body directly address this commitment:

   a. Continue to increase the number of academically talented students attending Our University, achieve by 1993 an average SAT score of 1200 for entering freshmen and maintain this SAT level as a minimum throughout the rest of the planning period.
   b. Continue to increase the number of out-of-state students attending Our University, so that this group will comprise 50% of the student body by 1993, and maintain this percentage as a minimum for the rest of the planning period.
   c. Give increased emphasis to recruitment of minority students (Hispanic, Black, Asian, and Native American) and increase their representation in the overall student population.

    d. Strive to have an equal number of men and women in the student body.

2. Each graduate of Our University will be treated as an individual, and all graduates of baccalaureate-level programs at the university will have developed a depth of understanding in their major field and been afforded the opportunity to prepare for a career or profession following graduation. Additionally, they will be able to

    a. Express themselves clearly, correctly, and succinctly in a written manner.

    b. Make an effective verbal presentation of their ideas concerning a topic.

    c. Read and offer an analysis of periodical literature concerning a topic of interest.

    d. Complete accurately basic mathematical calculations.

    e. Demonstrate a sufficient level of computer literacy.

F. *Academic Support Services*

Services in direct support of academic programs must be both effective and efficient in the accomplishment of their assigned activities. Our University will strive for excellence in the following goals:

1. Continue to increase library acquisitions so that the number of bound volumes will reach 650,000 by 1993.

2. Improve the quality of library materials supporting instruction by acquiring the most advanced audiovisual equipment and by judiciously purchasing periodicals applicable to a liberal arts and sciences curriculum, as well as the limited number of graduate programs offered.

3. Increase accessibility to computer facilities at the university for both students and faculty through expansion of microcomputer laboratories and enhancement of computer support.

4. Develop more systematic data concerning the outcome of each student's educational experiences.

5. Plan and modify the existing classroom and laboratory space to meet the evolving needs of the new curriculum.

III. STUDENT AFFAIRS

The functions of the Student Affairs Office are to establish an environment at Our University that supports and encourages students in their academic progress and to assist those students in their personal and social development. Student Affairs prepares Our University graduates for adult life by teaching them to appreciate quality, to develop values, to accept responsibility for their decisions and actions, and to know how and when to compromise.

To accomplish this mission, the following specific goals must receive continuing and expanded attention:

A. *Environment*
   1. Provide a comfortable and secure living environment in the residence halls.
   2. Encourage development of appropriate attitudes and conduct for a communal academic environment.
   3. Expand and encourage supplemental cultural and intellectual enrichment opportunities outside the classroom.
   4. Explore the possibility of offering more options in housing.
   5. Provide opportunities in an informal atmosphere for interaction of faculty with students outside the classroom.
   6. Include in the University Center, which is being reorganized, a bookstore offering excellent academic support materials and current literature, as well as appropriate notions, supplies, and services needed by students, faculty, and staff.
   7. Provide a variety of options for nutritional meals in comfortable and attractive settings for resident as well as commuting students, faculty, staff, and guests.

B. *Development*
   1. Offer opportunities for self-evaluation and self-knowledge through administration and interpretation of standardized tests.
   2. Provide comprehensive career planning for all students and career counseling for seniors and graduate students; prepare students to conduct effective job searches; and coordinate employment interviews on the campus.

IV. FISCAL AFFAIRS

The purpose of the University's Fiscal Affairs Office is to provide an environment that enables faculty, staff, and students to concentrate on their appropriate tasks, which are essentially educational.

Fiscal Affairs has two major areas of responsibility: (a) the management of, and accounting for, financial resources (the handling of funds, endowments, investments, and expenditures for salaries and wages); and (b) the operation of support services (physical plant, purchasing, security, personnel, and other areas). These two essential areas provide a base upon which the institution can accomplish its mission.

A. *Financial Resources*

1. To achieve expansion and growth in financial assets, Our University will
   a. Manage the budget prudently.
   b. Encourage and assist its faculty in seeking university-administered grants and contracts from external sources.
   c. Price its auxiliary enterprise services so that they are self-sustaining and do not draw from other resources of the institution.
2. In allocating funds for its academic and economic needs, the university will emphasize the following goals:
   a. Maintaining a level of salaries that will attract and retain competent professionals.
   b. Providing adequate funding for scholarships to attract exceptional students.
   c. Purchasing and replacing equipment in support of the instruction and research needs of the university.
   d. Building adequate plant-fund reserves in order to protect against deferred maintenance.

B. *Support Services*

1. To achieve maximum utilization of its resources, the university will
   a. Use its personnel, equipment, structures, and funds efficiently and effectively to provide a safe and comfortable environment for all faculty, staff, and students.
   b. Fund support services at a level that provides for the most efficient operation consistent with a scholarly environment.
2. In personnel matters, the university will
   a. Improve communications between support services and all employees to ensure that applicable fiscal and personnel procedures are understood.
   b. Maintain a vigorous affirmative action program which will include specific goals and a systematic review of procedures and progress.

V. UNIVERSITY RELATIONS AND DEVELOPMENT

The University Relations and Development Office manages the closely related areas of fund raising, alumni activities, and public relations. Most of the activities and programs take place for the ultimate purpose of increasing gift income for the university and attracting qualified students and faculty to the university.

Within this context, the University Relations and Development Office has established the following integrated goals:

A. *Fund Raising*
   1. Build a permanent university endowment of $150 million to $155 million by 1993.
   2. Achieve a level of annual giving (unrestricted annual fund) of at least $750,000 per year by 1993.
   3. Achieve 35% participation among alumni in the annual giving program.

B. *Alumni Activities*
   1. Have 5% of all alumni return to campus for various programs such as Alumni Weekend, Alumni College, class reunions, and so forth.
   2. Develop an active national alumni association with chapters in all cities where 100 or more alumni reside.

C. *Public Relations*
   1. Achieve a national image of the university as a high-quality, selective-admissions liberal arts and sciences institution that is among the best of its type in the nation.
   2. Maintain a positive relationship with the community in which the institution is located.

Examples of Linkage between Expanded Statement of Institutional Purpose, Departmental/Program Intended Outcomes/Objectives, and Assessment Criteria and Procedures

Accounting Degree Program

Example of Linkage between
Expanded Statement of Institutional Purpose,
Departmental/Program Intended Outcomes/Objectives, and
Assessment Criteria and Procedures at Our University

Expanded Statement of Institutional Purpose	**Departmental/Program Intended Outcomes/Objectives**	**Assessment Criteria & Procedures**
Mission Statement: The principal focus of Our University's curricular program is undergraduate education in the liberal arts and sciences, combined with a number of directly career related and preprofessional fields.	1. Students completing the baccalaureate program in accounting will be well prepared for their first position in the field.	a. Eighty percent of those taking the CPA exam each year and indicating an accounting degree from Our University will pass three of four parts on the exam.
Goal Statements: All graduates of baccalaureate programs will have developed a depth of understanding in their major field and been afforded the opportunity to prepare for a career following graduation.		b. Eighty-five percent of the graduates of the accounting baccalaureate program will "agree" or "strongly agree" with the statement "I am well prepared for my first position" contained in Our University's Graduating Student Questionnaire.
		c. Employers of accounting program graduates hired through the Our University Placement Service will indicate on a survey forwarded to them by the Placement Service one year after employment of the graduate, an average rating of 7.5 or more (on a scale of 1-10) in response to the question "How well was your employee prepared for his position by Our University?"
	2. Baccalaureate graduates of the accounting program will find ready employment in the field.	a. Ninety percent of accounting graduates registered with the placement service each fall will have received a job offer by the close of spring semester each year.
		b. Sixty percent of students completing the accounting degree program will indicate that they are currently employed or have accepted a job offer in their response to the Our University Graduating Student Questionnaire.
		c. Eighty percent of the accounting program graduates responding to the Our University Recent Alumni Survey will indicate that they are employed in a "directly career related" position.
	3. Graduates will be experienced in the use of microcomputers for accounting procedures.	a. Baccalaureate accounting program graduates will be required to complete successfully (as judged by a jury of faculty from the department) a major accounting project utilizing microcomputer applications during their last semester at the university.
		b. Seventy-five percent of accounting graduates will "agree" or "strongly agree" with the statement "I feel very comfortable in an automated accounting environment" on the Our University Graduating Student Questionnaire.

General Education Program

Example of Linkage between
Expanded Statement of Institutional Purpose, Departmental/Program Intended Outcomes/Objectives, and Assessment Criteria and Procedures at Our University

Expanded Statement of Institutional Purpose

Mission Statement: The principal focus of Our University's curricular program is undergraduate education in the liberal arts and sciences.

Goal Statements (related to baccalaureate graduates): Additionally, they will be able to

a. Express themselves clearly, correctly, and succinctly in a written manner.

Departmental/Program Intended Outcomes/Objectives

1. Prior to graduation each student will demonstrate general expository writing with correct grammar, punctuation, and spelling.

2. Graduates will have demonstrated their ability to organize and effectively express their thoughts in writing concerning a major issue of then current interest in their chosen field of study.

Assessment Criteria & Procedures

a. By the end of their junior year, all students will have placed on file in the Office of Career and Life Planning within the Our University Placement Service a 500-word essay outlining their career plans related to their courses of study. During each summer, the Director of the Freshman Writing Program will review these documents to determine whether they meet the standards of students completing the Freshman Writing Program. Those students whose career essays are judged unacceptable will be required to complete a one-semester Senior Writing Clinic during their next semester in enrollment, following which they will be required to submit another career essay for evaluation.

a. During the first semester of their senior year, each student will (separate from any course requirement) be required to submit to the appropriate academic department a minimum 5,000-word research/argumentative paper putting forward their position regarding a then current issue or problem in their primary field of study. Departmental juries of faculty will be convened to review each paper for its organization and assess the student's writing ability and knowledge in the field. Students will not be permitted to receive a degree until the appropriate department has certified acceptance of their research/argumentative paper.

Academic Affairs

Example of Linkage between
Expanded Statement of Institutional Purpose,
Departmental/Program Intended Outcomes/Objectives, and
Assessment Criteria and Procedures at Our University

**Expanded Statement of
Institutional Purpose**

Mission Statement: Our University also offers master's and doctoral degree programs in selected professional areas that will prepare individuals for positions of leadership in their chosen careers.

Goal Statement: Review current graduate-degree programs to determine the academic and economic feasibility of their continuation.

**Departmental/Program
Intended Outcomes/Objectives**

1. Specify criteria for graduate degree program review regarding academic and economic feasibility.

2. Following identification of criteria for review of graduate programs, data needed for each criteria will be calculated.

3. Based upon the criteria established and review of the data provided the Dean of the Graduate School (in conjunction with the Graduate Council) will recommend to the Vice President for Academic Affairs those graduate programs to be continued.

**Assessment Criteria
& Procedures**

a. By the end of academic year 1988-89, the Graduate School Dean will have submitted to the Vice President for Academic Affairs a list of criteria concerning academic and economic feasibility for use in graduate program review.

b. The Vice President for Academic Affairs will accept or modify the suggested criteria by the beginning of academic year 1989-90.

a. The Office of Institutional Research will identify specific data relating to each specified criterion by the end of fall semester 1989-90.

b. By the end of the 1989-90 spring semester, the Office of Institutional Research will have completed calculations providing the specific data identified regarding each criteria for each graduate program at the university.

c. Comparative data concerning graduate programs at comparable institutions, where available, will be provided by the Office of Institutional Research.

d. All institutional and comparative data will be received by the Dean of the Graduate School by the beginning of fall semester 1990-91.

a. The Vice President for Academic Affairs will have received the Dean of the Graduate School's recommendations by the end of spring semester 1990-91.

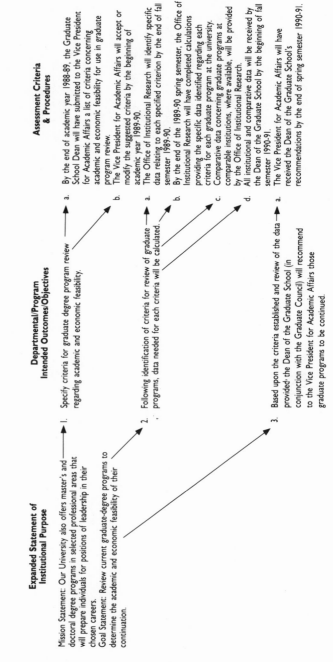

Department of Continuing Education

Example of Linkage between
Expanded Statement of Institutional Purpose,
Departmental/Program Intended Outcomes/Objectives, and
Assessment Criteria and Procedures at Our University

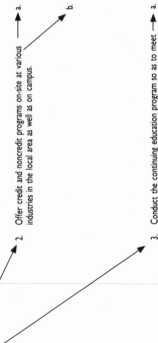

Expanded Statement of Institutional Purpose

Mission Statement: In addition, recognizing its responsibility to the larger community, Our University provides a variety of carefully selected programs of continuing education and cultural enrichment.

Goal Statements: Be responsive to the continuing education needs of local businesses and industries in areas in which Our University is academically strong.

Departmental/Program Intended Outcomes/Objectives

1. Identify the continuing education needs of local businesses and industries.

2. Offer credit and noncredit programs on-site at various industries in the local area as well as on campus.

3. Conduct the continuing education program so as to meet its own costs or generate excess revenue.

Assessment Criteria & Procedures

a. During academic year 1989-90, the Our University Department of Continuing Education will have conducted a needs survey of local businesses and industries to identify unmet needs for continuing education support.

b. By the close of academic year 1989-90, the results of the needs survey will have been utilized to identify a limited number of opportunities for continuing education activities servicing local businesses and industries.

a. In academic year 1990-91 and each year thereafter, the Department of Continuing Education will be able to identify a minimum of twenty-five continuing education programs (credit or noncredit) during that year conducted on-site at various local businesses and industries.

b. In academic year 1990-91 and each year thereafter, the Our University Chief Academic Officer will be able to identify a minimum of 10 on-campus courses (during the fall and spring semesters combined) that have been scheduled during the late afternoon, evening, or on Saturday in response to needs expressed by local businesses and industries for continuing professional education for their employees.

a. Annual comparison of expenditures for the Department of Continuing Education with revenue from all sources generated by that unit will indicate at least a break-even relationship each fiscal year.

Student Services

Example of Linkage between
Expanded Statement of Institutional Purpose,
Departmental/Program Intended Outcomes/Objectives, and
Assessment Criteria and Procedures at Our University

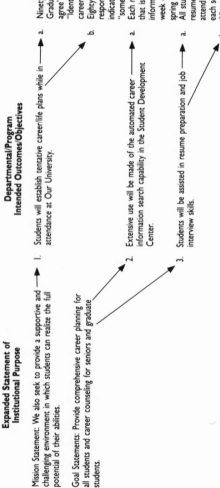

Expanded Statement of Institutional Purpose	Departmental/Program Intended Outcomes/Objectives	Assessment Criteria & Procedures
Mission Statement: We also seek to provide a supportive and challenging environment in which students can realize the full potential of their abilities. Goal Statements: Provide comprehensive career planning for all students and career counseling for seniors and graduate students.	1. Students will establish tentative career/life plans while in attendance at Our University.	a. Ninety percent of respondents to the Our University Graduating Student Survey will "agree" or "strongly agree" with the statement that while in attendance each "identified my career interests and formulated long-term career and life goals." b. Eighty percent of the Graduating Student Questionnaire respondents who have already secured employment will indicate that the employment is either "directly" or "somewhat" related to their major.
	2. Extensive use will be made of the automated career information search capability in the Student Development Center.	a. Each microcomputer in the Student Development Center that is equipped with an automated career search and/or information package will average at least 25 hours per week of student use of that package during the fall and spring semesters combined.
	3. Students will be assisted in resume preparation and job interview skills.	a. All students will be offered the opportunity to attend a resume workshop, and 30% of the graduating seniors will attend such a workshop or receive separate assistance each semester. b. All students will be offered the opportunity to attend an interviewing skills workshop and "mock interview" during their senior year, and 10% of the graduating class will attend.

Admissions Office

Example of Linkage between
Expanded Statement of Institutional Purpose,
Departmental/Program Intended Outcomes/Objectives, and
Assessment Criteria and Procedures at Our University

Expanded Statement of Institutional Purpose	Departmental/Program Intended Outcomes/Objectives	Assessment Criteria & Procedures
Mission Statement: Our University is to provide an outstanding education for a relatively small number of talented and highly motivated students from a diversity of geographic, ethnic, and socioeconomic backgrounds. Goal Statements: Continue to increase the number of academically talented students attending Our University; achieve by 1993 an average SAT score for entering freshmen of 1200, and maintain this level, as a minimum, throughout the rest of the planning period.	1. The proportion of the entering freshman class with SAT averages between 1325 and 1350 will be increased by focusing merit scholarship offers in this range. 2. Applicants for admission with an SAT score less than 1100 will not be eligible for financial aid from university funds. 3. The proportion of each entering freshman class composed of National Merit finalists will increase each year.	a. Review of the entering freshman class profile provided by the Office of Institutional Research each fall semester will indicate an increase in the proportion of entering students with SAT scores in the 1325-1350 range each year. b. Analysis of the merit scholarship offers made by the university each year to entering freshmen will indicate at least twice the proportion of offers to students in the 1325-1350 SAT range as in other 25-point SAT ranges. a. Analysis of the Financial Aid Office annual report will not indicate offers of university-funded financial aid to entering students with an SAT score of less than 1100. a. Review of the entering freshman class profile each year will indicate a continued increase in the number of National Merit finalists each year as well as the proportion that they comprise of Our University's entering freshman class.

Computer Center

Example of Linkage between
Expanded Statement of Institutional Purpose,
Departmental/Program Intended Outcomes/Objectives, and
Assessment Criteria and Procedures at Our University

**Expanded Statement of
Institutional Purpose**

Mission Statement: We also seek to provide a supportive and challenging environment in which students can realize the full potential of their abilities.

Goal Statements: All graduates of baccalaureate level programs at the university will be able to

a. . . . d

e.   Demonstrate a sufficient level of computer literacy.

**Departmental/Program
Intended Outcomes/Objectives**

1.   Make mainframe and microcomputer support readily accessible on the campus.

2.   Support integration of computer-assisted instruction (CAI) into classes.

3.   Provide a wide variety of elementary programming languages and user-friendly software packages.

**Assessment Criteria
& Procedures**

a.   Either a terminal to the mainframe or a microcomputer will be found in each classroom building or dormitory on the campus.

b.   All faculty requesting computer access will have been provided either a terminal to the mainframe or a microcomputer.

c.   Access to the campus microcomputer laboratory will be made available between 8:00 A.M. and 12:00 P.M. seven days per week during the fall and spring semesters.

a.   Current CAI software will be available in the computer center.

b.   Five percent of the faculty will have attended a CAI workshop presented by the Our University Computer Center each year.

a.   Access through either the mainframe or microcomputer laboratory to Pascal, Basic, APL, and/or PLI will be provided to students in each introductory programming class.

b.   Current word-processing and spread-sheet packages will be readily available to students and faculty through the mainframe, microcomputer laboratory, or computer terminals/facilities in each dormitory and faculty office.

Sponsored Research

Example of Linkage between
Expanded Statement of Institutional Purpose,
Departmental/Program Intended Outcomes/Objectives, and
Assessment Criteria and Procedures at Our University

Expanded Statement of Institutional Purpose	Departmental/Program Intended Outcomes/Objectives	Assessment Criteria & Procedures
Mission Statement: Our University recognizes its responsibility in maintaining a position of excellence and leadership in research.	1. The majority of the research proposals for external funding forwarded through the Office of the Associate Vice Chancellor for Research and Dean of the Graduate School will be directly linked to local or regional (within this state) industries.	a. Each proposal for externally funded research will be accompanied by a one-page transmittal sheet explaining if and how the proposal relates to a local or regional industry. At the end of the fiscal year, the transmittal sheets will be reviewed, and 50% or more will be judged as directly linked to local or regional industries by the Our University Research Board.
Goal Statements: Our University will seek during the next five years to	2. The proportion of those proposals for external funding that are directly linked to local or regional industries and are funded will substantially exceed all other such proposals submitted.	a. Following annual identification of those research grant proposals directly linked with local or regional industries, analysis of actual funding will reveal that twice the proportion of such proposals, compared to all proposals submitted, receive funding.
1. . . 3		
4. Focus the development of proposals for externally funded or organized research on subjects directly related to local/regional industries or those subjects of particular interest to foundations with which Our University has enjoyed a continuing relationship.	3. Local industries will be aware of Our University's efforts to seek funding in research areas related to their fields.	a. Of those proposals for external funding identified as being directly linked with local or regional industries, half or more will include a letter of support, endorsement, or cooperation from the appropriate local or regional industry.
		b. Half of those CEOs of major local industries responding to a letter from Our University's CEO (25% sample each year) will be able to identify research performed by Our University that has been directly related to their products.

Physical Plant

Example of Linkage between
Expanded Statement of Institutional Purpose,
Departmental/Program Intended Outcomes/Objectives, and
Assessment Criteria and Procedures at Our University

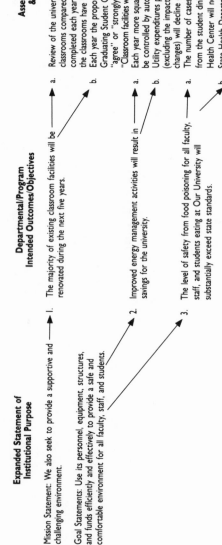

Expanded Statement of Institutional Purpose

Mission Statement: We also seek to provide a supportive and challenging environment.

Goal Statements: Use its personnel, equipment, structures, and funds efficiently and effectively to provide a safe and comfortable environment for all faculty, staff, and students.

Departmental/Program Intended Outcomes/Objectives

1. The majority of existing classroom facilities will be renovated during the next five years.

2. Improved energy management activities will result in savings for the university.

3. The level of safety from food poisoning for all faculty, staff, and students eating at Our University will substantially exceed state standards.

Assessment Criteria & Procedures

a. Review of the university's inventory of general purpose classrooms compared to its list of renovation projects completed each year will indicate that at least 10% of the classrooms have been renovated each year.

b. Each year the proportion of respondents to the Graduating Student Questionnaire indicating that they "agree" or "strongly agree" with the statement "Classroom facilities were conducive to learning" will increase.

a. Each year more square feet of space at the university will be controlled by automated energy management systems.

b. Utility expenditures per square foot in existing structures (excluding the impact of rate increases and structural changes) will decline each year.

a. The number of cases of food poisoning (possibly resulting from the student dining halls) reported to the Student Health Center will not exceed two per year.

b. State Health Department inspections of campus food-service facilities will indicate an average score at least 10 points (on a scale of 100) above the average for commercial establishments in the city.

Two-Year College
Business Transfer Program

Example of Linkage between
Expanded Statement of Institutional Purpose,
Departmental/Program Intended Outcomes/Objectives, and
Assessment Criteria and Procedures at Our University

**Expanded Statement of
Institutional Purpose**

To provide students in the college's transfer program with courses that are accepted at leading four-year institutions and that provide a sufficient foundation for successful completion of more advanced courses at a four-year institution and ultimate completion of a baccalaureate degree.

**Departmental/Program
Intended Outcomes/Objectives**

1. Students transferring to a four-year college in the field of accounting will find their Accounting 101-102 at this two-year college fully accepted as the basis for Accounting 201-202 at a four-year institution.

2. Most of the students completing Accounting 101-102 at this two-year college who major in business at a four-year college will successfully (grade "C" or better) pass Accounting 201-202 at their four-year institution.

3. Students completing the two-year course of study leading toward transfer to a four-year college in the field of business will complete their baccalaureate degree at almost the same rate as those students originally enrolling at the four-year college.

**Assessment Criteria
& Procedures**

a. Ninety percent of those business students responding to a follow-up survey one year after transfer to a four-year institution will respond that their Accounting 101-102 courses taken at the two-year college were fully accepted by the four-year college.

b. An annual spot check of 25% of the two-year college's primary transfer institutions will reveal that they indicate full acceptance of Accounting 101-102 taken at the two-year college as a prerequisite for Accounting 201-202 at their institution.

a. Analysis of data received by the two-year college concerning grades in specific courses made by its graduates at each four-year institution will indicate that greater than 50% of its graduates who took Accounting 101-102 at the two-year college and majored in a business-related field at the four-year college made a grade of "C" or higher at the four-year college in Accounting 201-202.

b. More than 50% of the two-year college's transfer graduates who are majoring in business at a four-year institution will report making a grade of "C" or higher in Accounting 201-202.

a. Analysis of data received by the two-year college concerning its transfer students' grades, and so forth, at each four-year college will reveal graduation rates in the field of business by its transfer students at 85% or higher of the rate for students originally admitted at the four-year institution.

Two-Year College
Occupational/Technical Program

Example of Linkage between
Expanded Statement of Institutional Purpose,
Departmental/Program Intended Outcomes/Objectives, and
Assessment Criteria and Procedures at Our University

Expanded Statement of Institutional Purpose	Departmental/Program Intended Outcomes/Objectives	Assessment Criteria & Procedures
To offer educational opportunities that are occupationally oriented and lead to being successfully employed in a semi-professional or skilled position at the end of the program of instruction.	1. Graduates of the Automotive Technician Program will be successfully employed in the field.	a. Fifty percent of the graduates of the Automotive Technician Program will report employment in the field on the Graduating Student Survey administered at the time of course completion.
		b. Eighty percent of the graduates of the Automotive Technician Program will report employment in the field on the Recent Alumni Survey distributed one year after graduation.
	2. Graduates of the Automotive Technician Program will be technically proficient.	a. At the close of their final term, 90% of the graduates will be able to identify and correct within a given period of time all of the mechanical problems in five test cars which have been "prepared" for the students by automotive department faculty.
		b. Eighty percent of the Automotive Technician Program graduates will pass the National Automotive Test.
	3. Employers of the Automotive Technician Program graduates will be pleased with the education received by their employees.	a. Eighty percent of the automotive respondents to an Employer Survey conducted every three years by the college will respond that they would be pleased to employ future graduates of the Automotive Technician Program.
		b. Fifty percent of the automotive employers registered with the College Placement Service will make at least one offer to a graduate of the Automotive Technician Program each year.

Subject Index